The Complete Book of

FLOWERS *and* PLANTS

for Interior Decoration

THE COMPLETE BOOK OF
FLOWERS *and* PLANTS
FOR INTERIOR DECORATION

ESTHER WHEELER and ANABEL COMBS LASKER
Revised by ANABEL COMBS LASKER

ASSISTED BY BARBARA BAER, MEMBER, A.I.D.

Drawings by Janet Porto

Hearthside Press Inc.   Publishers

New York

ACKNOWLEDGMENTS

We are indebted to:

The flower arrangers who made the arrangements which appear in these pages. A special debt is owed those whose work, because of insufficient information available to us, must remain anonymous; Federated Garden Clubs of New York State, Inc., and its Life Members; the Garden Club of America; and the Horticultural Society of New York; the ladies who so graciously opened their homes for photography; Paul Frese for the list of annuals; Mrs. W. H. Barton, Chairman Flower Show Schools, National Council of State Garden Clubs, Inc., for "The Placement Show"; Marguerite Palmer, *Houston Press* and Mrs. S. H. Lambden, Natchez, Mississippi, for historical data; T. H. Everett, Horticulturist and Curator of Education, New York Botanical Garden, for his help with Chapter 6; Mrs. Louise B. Fisher, Williamsburg Restoration; and Nedda C. Anders of Hearthside Press whose unsparing efforts and help have made this book a reality.

1. *(Frontis) In a tiny back hall which furniture would crowd, a hanging mirror above a wall shelf reflects the open door leading to a garden, and a colorful arrangement of spring flowers. Stock, tulips, anemones and a few begonia leaves are secured on a pinholder in a large teapot on a trivet with appropriate accessories. Arranged by Mrs. Robert C. Lawrence, Jr. (Photo by Hugelmeyer)*

To my beloved mother, Mrs. Lee Combs Sr., whose inspiration and teaching have been a rule for life.

Anabel Combs Lasker

To Mary Ridgely Mackey, Executive Director, National Plant, Flower and Fruit Guild, for her lifetime devotion to garden club work.

Esther Wheeler

CONTENTS

2. *Dramatic impact is achieved with a handsome water garden built into an elegant entrance hall. Papyrus, appropriate to the simple modern décor, can be bought at nurseries featuring aquatic plant material and can also be grown in pots. Large window areas assure a maximum of direct sunlight. Interior design by Cannell & Chaffin. (Photo by George R. Szanik)*

I

Flowers for every home

FLOWERS HAVE ADORNED INTERIORS FOR HUN-
dreds of years. They surpass all other decoration in giving individuality to home settings,
for there is infinite variety in their form, color,
and seasonal growth. Since flowers have been
used for their beauty and for pleasing decorative arrangements for so long, you might
wonder why this book should be necessary.
Yet so far as we know, there is no other book
in print that will show you how to select
flowers and containers that will be appropri-
ately tied in with the style and materials of
the newer types of home decoration, or with
combinations of old and new styles.

Today homeowners are very much aware
of contemporary design. They have a well-
developed sense of color and an overwhelm-
ing urge in the face of mass production to give
their homes a special imprint. This still-grow-
ing interest has made potential flower arrangers of almost everyone, in apartment or
house or considering decoration of a new
home.

FUNCTIONAL AND DECORATIVE
USES OF FLOWERS

In today's "open plan" home, and in many
older ones remodeled in a similar manner,
planters are often built into floors and wells
to serve functionally as room dividers or to
give textural interest to plain wall surfaces.
Furniture designers, too, are providing planter
pockets in tables, lamps, and wall brackets.
The tailored quality of modern furniture
needs the softening influence that flowers
bring to a room. In such décor, flowers are
not considered just extra decoration but are
a fundamental part of the interior.

Flowers are the least expensive way to
decorate, and if decorating mistakes are made,
they are the easiest and least expensive to correct. Young married couples with a limited
budget and a dollar or two to spend on exotic
greens from the florist can fill a bare spot for
months, using the foliage fresh at first, later
dried.

3.   *No haphazard grouping of flowers could produce the effect of unity which characterizes this thoughtfully planned composition. The foliage in the print and the living arrangement seem to flow from one another. The large rose at the right directs the eye to the luster mug, thus skilfully making it a part of the whole design. Arranged by Fred Morley. (Photo by Gottscho-Schleisner)*

A mass of flowers will unify all the colors in a room, hide an unattractive wall jog, and conceal spotted wallpaper or even an unsightly radiator. Even a dark hall, too small to hold furniture, can be made attractive with bright yellow flowers in a wall planter, lavabo, or other hanging planter.

PLANNING ENHANCES THE CHARM OF FLOWERS

But must flowers be arranged? Aren't they just as lovely "stuck in a vase"? Undeniably, flowers have intrinsic beauty, which may be displayed in any garden, but who can deny that the most successful gardens are those that are well planned? Indoors or out, design and construction enhance the basic charm of floral material. Compositions that please the eye of every beholder, even those who are trained in design, are rarely accidental.

Handsome arrangements are within the ability of every amateur who can follow simple directions. Chapter II, for example, will help you relate flowers to the style of your home. Chapter V will explain the mechanics of putting your design together. A few simple tools, space for containers, a place to work (it need not be as elaborate as the one in Plate 4), and you are on the way to becoming a flower arranger!

4. *Good decoration provides plenty of room for the needs of the family. Here a basement has been attractively planned for a few hobbies, a few chores. Built-in shelves and drawers hold containers, accessories, equipment, and books. Running water necessary for conditioning flowers is nearby. (Courtesy of Armstrong Linoleum Co.)*

5. *A flower arrangement never fails to add interest to a room, as these two views show. Note flatness of perspective in this. In the home of Mrs. Millard Rothenberg. (Photo by Gottscho-Schleisner)*

6. *A spring arrangement of forced apple blossoms, lilacs and magnolias, in a fine porcelain vase, in a triangular design. Arranged by Anabel Combs Lasker. (Photo by Gottscho-Schleisner)*

II

Harmonizing flowers and containers with period styles

RARELY HAS DECORATING BEEN AS RICH AND EN- joyable an art as it is today. Fabrics and furniture designed with an eye on the past make possible home settings from every age. For elegance, your home may take its theme from the French Empire, for classic formality from eighteenth-century England, or for country simplicity from the rural arts of the Pennsylvania Dutch.

With such a wealth of ideas to choose from, you may combine periods in your furniture and accessories, but they must have the effect of loving collection rather than of wholesale purchase. Combining must also be done with knowledge lest a hodgepodge result. In the past, styles in furniture and flowers frequently developed along the same lines. During the Regency, for example, a return to classic formality in decoration was similarly expressed in the use of arrangements that had classic symmetrical balance and proportion. Today, Japanese influence on contemporary life is paralleled in architecture, furniture, and floral art, all emphasizing form, linear pattern, subtle color, and symbolism rather than strong contrast, ornamentation, and massed effect.

These examples point out how expressive flower decoration can be. When you learn how plant material has been used in the past, you will have studied the culture of mankind. When making a simple herb bouquet for your Early American kitchen, you will be aware that it is not only aesthetic but appropriate in period style. Yet it is not necessary to copy only authentic arrangements. Once you have the feeling of the period style, you can change and adapt it as you wish. To help you harmonize all the furnishings and ornaments in your home is the aim of this chapter.

GREEK AND ROMAN HERITAGE

The ancient Greeks were by nature a people so dedicated to beauty that their art has lived through the ages. They left us a heritage of simplicity and grace that has never been surpassed. Starting with simple almost geometric forms, all of which were brought into a harmonious unit, they tempered these forms by observing nature and making their works of art a little more than what the eye actually

7. *This French Directoire dining room contains such suitable ornaments as two tole urns and a massed flower arrangement on the mantel. The arrangement of fruit in a basket is typically French. Arranged by Mrs. Donald V. Lowe and Mrs. Richard S. Russel. (Photo by Hugelmeyer)*

sees. In interior decoration today, their symbols of the acanthus leaf, egg-and-dart, and key and scroll are constantly being used in architecture and in the home. Wreaths, swags, and garlands using the lily, rose, crocus, violet, acanthus, daisy, olive, narcissus, iris, laurel, ivy, and other plants were also their contribution.

EARLY EUROPEAN PERIODS

GOTHIC AND RENAISSANCE STYLES

In contrast with the disciplined formality of the classic Greek and Roman styles, the medieval period produced the romantic Gothic style. Gothic furniture would seem to have little relation to modern design, yet one might say that the earliest built-ins were Gothic chests, consoles, and window seats. Wood, richly decorated with gilt, polychrome, ivory, and metal brought richness to great stone castles. The designs of the medieval tapestries, hung on otherwise barren walls, are filled with simple flowers—buttercups, ferns, ivy, parsley, and thistles. The slender tapered arch, familiar to us in church buildings, influenced many designers including Chippendale. Today, the beautiful and intricate needlework and massive custom-made furniture pieces built into magnificent modern homes, frequently illustrated in home magazines, are a reminder of this earlier style.

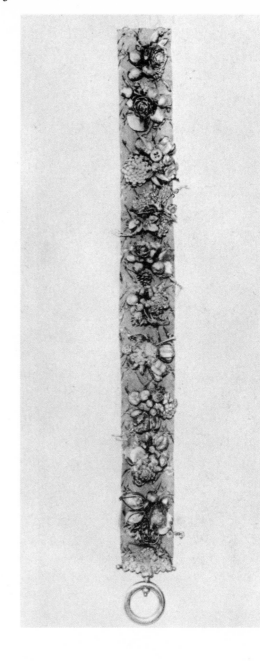

8. *A replica of an eighteenth century bell pull is made of gilded dried seed pods and cones secured with fine wire to figured silk which first had been stitched to cardboard. (Procedure is given in Chapter 5). The ring at the bottom is antique brass. The drawing illustrates the ornamental pull in a French Provincial library. When the available space is too small for a picture grouping, a narrow design such as this, or an arrangement in a tall vase of long-stemmed flowers which have more line than mass weight, is ideal. Arranged by Esther Wheeler. (Photo by Gottscho-Schleisner)*

9. *Where elegance is appropriate, as in a Georgian setting, fine accessories, smooth textures and well groomed flowers are in harmony with the formal interior. Arranged by Constance Spry. (Photo by Cowderey & Moss Ltd.)*

In the Gothic influence during the Middle Ages, a rebirth of interest in ornamental beauty and proportions produced the style known as Renaissance. Interiors were enlivened with rich designs of fruits, vines, and flowers in garlands, swags, and della Robbia wreaths. Gilded swags, bell pulls, and scrolls of seed pods, nuts, and glycerinized foliage in symmetrical balance, and delicately massed flowers such as delphinium, roses, tulips, sweet sultan, anemones, iris, and lilies in silver bowls and urns are typical of this period and characterized by good taste.

OPULENT FRENCH PERIOD STYLES

In France, in the eighteenth century, begins an era that directly concerns present-day furniture styles. The voluptuous baroque curve replaced the lovely symmetry of the Renaissance style, and the era of opulence in decorating was ushered in. The zenith of ornamentation was reached perhaps under Louis XV, in whose reign the rococo style flourished. Although frequently used as a synonym for baroque, rococo is actually lighter in scale, more intimate and human. Flowing curves that reverse themselves are typical.

While the amazingly ornate rooms of the styles of Louis XIV, XV, XVI would be inappropriate today, individual pieces from these opulent reigns can add luxury to any modern home. Fine petit point chairs, ornamental coffee tables with painted scenes, marble ornamental mantels with Sèvres fruit plaques and flower swags are available in modern copies if not always in genuine antiques. Plain or striped satins are typical, tufted velvets, brocades, silks and damasks (many available today in practical synthetics) used in upholstery or window covering, with fringe and tassel, in swags or draperies, will give this opulent air to your home. Delicate colors of apricot, gold, light and dark green, pink, striped white and blue, pale yellow and lavender have made the French style particularly suitable in boudoirs, where opulence and luxury are desirable.

10.   *An entrance hall in the English Regency period reflects the dignity of the style. Fresh foliage in the lavabo, on the hall chest, and in the niche on the stairway, offer contrast to the magnificent appointments. In the home of Mr. and Mrs. James Ryder, Richard Plumer, Interior Decorator.*

LOUIS XV: *(left to right) Bergère; Fireplace and screen; Desk; Candelabrum; Epergne; Cache pot; Shell dish*

FLOWERS AND CONTAINERS IN FRENCH COURT STYLE

Elaborate porcelain pieces of Sèvres, Dresden, and bisque, containers of crystal with bronze and chaste silver, or mother-of-pearl inlaid with jewels will help you reproduce the French court style. Carved ivory and Chinese jars, and French bronze, Venetian glass, or porcelain urns with ormolu trimmings also may be used. Scalloped shell forms, lions, rams, masks, as well as ancient weapons, typical of the more regal earlier period, were hung on the walls and garlanded with flowers, hearts, musical instruments, ribbons, and, above all, cupids. You can capture the spirit of the period in a loose, airy delicately massed arrangement using poppies, larkspur, carnations, iris, and roses combined with ivy tendrils and stressing a delicate crescent curve or S line.

For a Louis XVI room, use a silver or glass French epergne filled with mounds of small fruit, such as lady apples, kumquats, small pears, and strawberries. Let small bunches of green grapes with self foliage or small ivy leaves hang over the sides of the container. The leafy top of a pineapple can be used for height.

For a French music room, a small porcelain or gilded violin may be used as a container for flowers, placing a pinholder in a hollowed-out section of its top. Use a horizontal line arrangement of snapdragons, tuberoses, carnations, and carnation foliage. Pastel ribbons may be festooned on the neck of the violin.

Other typical arrangements are candlesticks garlanded with flowers, using styrofoam wired to the arms and impaled with long-lasting flowers. A lovely carafe filled with amber liquid may be placed beside a plate of fresh fruit and a bowl of flowers. Fill shells with delicate short-stemmed flowers, such as violets, sweetheart roses, and pansies.

IMPORTS FROM CHINA CREATE CHINOISERIE

During the reign of Louis XIV, porcelains, paper hangings, and furniture were being imported from China. The attempt to duplicate these designs created the style of chinoiserie as a trend in decoration. While a contemporary designer, Chippendale, sought seriously to reproduce the perfection of Oriental design, the French were play-acting. As seen through the eyes of the French court, Chinese design was translated into furniture decorated with tortoise shell, mother-of-pearl inlay, and lacquering. Many modern pieces in chinoiserie are available in cabinets and tables and in contemporary printed fabrics and wall coverings. No modern decorator is

11. *Charming for a chest, this contemporary version of an Early American arrangement contains daffodils, daisies, tulips and geranium leaves, dried cockscomb, strawflowers, gypsophila and yarrow in an antique salt glaze pitcher with two nectarines as accessories. Arranged by Esther Wheeler and Anabel Combs Lasker. (Photo by Hugelmeyer)*

likely to fill a house with examples of chinoiserie, but as accent pieces they are unusual and interesting.

Knowing something of the relation of China to eighteenth-century France, it becomes apparent how suitable to French Provincial rooms is an accent of chinoiserie. If an arrangement in this style is wanted for a lacquered table, consider a Chinese celadon bowl on a lacquer stand with a few camellias or floated lotus flowers for a room of French inspiration.

12.   *An Early American cobbler's bench used as a coffee table holds cut geraniums and their own foliage in a pewter compote. The carved bird decoy repeats the design. Lilliput zinnias or nasturtiums could be substituted for the plant material used. Arranged by Anabel Combs Lasker, in the home of Mrs. William Herrmann. (Photo by Gottscho-Schleisner)*

FRENCH PROVINCIAL FLOWERS AND CONTAINERS

The painted Louis court styles had little place in the life of the bourgeois French in the provinces. Graceful fruitwood pieces scaled for smaller rooms furnished the country atmosphere. Such pieces are charming, comfortable, and adaptable. Dressed up with damask, needlepoint, brocades, or leathers, or used in a simpler tempo with gingham, self-hued toile prints with small repeats and coarsely woven linens, French Provincial is very adaptable to our contemporary way of life. The colors associated with this type of decoration are soft French blue, red, grayed pink, and medium ocher. However, the furniture has enough character to be used with more vivid and modern colors. Documentary prints and Early American small geometric patterns are suitable.

For the country home today, accessories that stem directly from local French craftsmen are most appropriate. Pewter, brass, copper, wrought iron, tin and tole, pottery including the distinctive Quimper ware, roughly carved wood, bark, and driftwood can be imaginative containers.

Fruit and vegetables, wheat and garden flowers, sweetly scented shrubs, violets and woodland flowers, geraniums, anemones, cyclamen, and lily of the valley are proper. Forced branches of chestnut, apple, and peach carry out provincial simplicity in a pewter or bronze container on a fruitwood sideboard. For the dress-up French Provincial room, use candlesticks, perhaps Baccarat glass or bronze with French blue candles, and a Lalique glass or bronze bowl with pink roses, ivy, and carnations.

FRENCH PROVINCIAL: *(left to right) Chair; Server with tureen; Lavabo table; Bed in alcove; Lamp; Basket; Geometric fabric*

FRENCH DIRECTOIRE AND EMPIRE STYLES

The French Directoire and Empire styles were more formal decorating periods, straight in line, rich in material, and fascinating in imagery. They were strongly influenced by ancient Greece and Rome, and from the excavation of Pompeii, architects and cabinetmakers seized on the Roman column and eagle, the laurel and acanthus leaf, the masks of Greek drama, urns and tripods, and the lyre as motifs. As Napoleon rose in power, his conquests were symbolized by rosettes, honeysuckle, anthemion, sphinxes, pyramids, obelisks, and lotus.

Because appearance counted more than comfort in this period, French Directoire is now more frequently used in sophisticated hallways, formal living rooms, and other places where one does not linger. The bold bright colors, however, as well as striped papers and interesting accessories, make this an attractive period from which to borrow.

The color combinations are Empire green with large areas of white and accents of black; yellow and white with touches of black; ruby red, royal blue, purple, or the Pompeian colors of olive green; old gold, yellow, and terra cotta with white and contrasted with black.

EMPIRE-DIRECTOIRE: *(left to right) Chair; Napoleon's bed; Swan table (Empress Josephine's symbol); Candelabrum; Empress bench; Urn; Obelisk*

FLOWERS AND CONTAINERS FOR DIRECTOIRE AND EMPIRE

Accessories included brass and bronze candlesticks, lamps of tole, triple brass, and bronze with classic columns or urns. Classic Roman busts on marble stands, bronze jardinieres, massive mantel clocks, and porcelain urns were used.

Directoire or Empire containers for flowers may be selected from the many authentic reproductions of bronze and porcelain urns on marble pedestals or from metal jardinieres or woven baskets. Bases may be either marble or alabaster. Accessories and vases trimmed with ormolu mounts (gilt French bronze) or their replicas are typical. Dramatic effects can be obtained with a white arrangement, brilliant yellow accent, in a black container.

The use of foliage and garlanding of flowers is particularly effective when the container is placed on a marble pedestal. Blackened magnolia leaves wired into a lyre design in an ornamental bronze urn with an accent of brilliant red roses would fit the style.

Plant materials suitable for this period are those which have classical associations or reflect Directoire simplicity: ivy and laurel leaves, wheat, roses, gladiolus, lily of the valley, anemones, bachelor buttons, hemerocallis, and the calla lily. Fruits such as pomegranates, grapes, peaches, and plums suggest the agrarian society of the Greeks.

ENGLISH PERIOD STYLES

Protestant refugees from Flanders brought with them to England the crafts of their native land. Furniture and still life paintings show the effect of their baroque C and S curves. In furniture, curves replaced the straight and massive lines of Jacobean and Tudor oak. In flowers, the work of the Flemish painter Peter Casteels in *Twelve Months of Fruit and Flowers* illustrates massed arrangements with a variety of plant material used in voluptuous oval and rectangular patterns, direct antecedents of the English and American Georgian styles.

The English styles of William and Mary and of Queen Anne were said to be the first in which royal furniture was made livable, but not until the reign of the four Georges was furniture designed that we would recognize today. Chippendale, Hepplewhite, the brothers Adam, and Thomas Sheraton represent the golden age of English cabinet design.

EARLY GEORGIANS—
CHIPPENDALE AND HEPPLEWHITE

Chippendale styles had four phases. The earliest was a continuation of Queen Anne; the second was influenced by the furniture of Louis XV; the third was Chinese inspired; and in the fourth, the Gothic arch was the motif. But in each style Chippendale had inimitable touches of his own. His Chinese phase is the one most reproduced in our homes today. It is a fine example of the way periods merge, since Chinese Chippendale is a clear link with French chinoiserie.

The best design motifs of this Chippendale style are flowers, fretwork, pagoda tops, and bamboo frames. The colors were much brighter than those of Louis XV, the comparable French period. Saffron yellow, lacquer red, turquoise, blue-green, brown and gold intensified the richness and sophistication of Chinese Chippendale rooms. Beautiful wallpapers and murals of Chinese gardens were used on one wall with the other three walls left plain. Silk and velvet fabrics or French *toile de Jouy*, a cotton fabric with delightful pastoral designs and printed in one color on a cream background, were favorites.

Accessories for a room in which Chinese Chippendale is predominant might include carved teakwood, mirrored stands, fans and ginger jars, Chinese tole and porcelain pots, bronzes, pewters, and lacquered work. Baskets with tree peonies, round bowls with narcissus, tall monochrome vases filled with branches of the ginkgo tree, hydrangeas, and tiger lilies are suitable for this period. Fruits —persimmons, peaches, pears, plums, quinces —may be used with these compositions.

George Hepplewhite had a lighter, more delicate style than Chippendale and a preference for curves. He did much to popularize the sideboard, giving it a serpentine curve with concave corners. Spode or Wedgwood bowls, or low boat-shaped pieces of Chelsea-Derby porcelain filled with roses or peonies make charming arrangements for a Hepplewhite sideboard. Elegance in form and color, soft grays, blue-greens, and pale yellows are typical.

13. *A charming table in an Early American room holds an arrangement of marigolds and asters in a wooden knife box lined with metal. The turkey print and other accessories are in the same tempo. Arranged by Anabel Combs Lasker, in the home of Mrs. William Herrmann. (Photo by Gottscho-Schleisner)*

LATER GEORGIANS—ADAM AND SHERATON

With Robert Adam, architect to King George III, classic Greek and Roman influences entered England in the period known as late Georgian. The four Adam brothers, all architects, were concerned with pieces in which architectural treatment was important. From them came rooms with tall niches for sculpture and classical urns, wonderful areas for flower arrangements.

Robert Adam gradually introduced satinwood and classical motifs, such as the acanthus leaf and honeysuckle, ram's head, winged griffin and lion, laurel garland and urn. Adam's carvings suggest arrangements for Georgian rooms quite literally, since they include such designs as a basket filled with plums, pomegranates, and peaches.

Sheraton designs are small, delicate, and sturdy. His writing desks, card tables, and sideboards echo these qualities. Sheraton's use of caning in chairs and settees makes these sparse upholstered pieces most elegant in modern rooms, and his colors, such as robin's-egg blue and white, have been brought back today with enthusiasm.

Your floral decoration for the Georgian period is delightfully flexible, because it was inspired from so many sources. Georgian motifs that invite repetition are plums, wheat, roses, honeysuckle, and pineapple. Swags, wreaths, and garlands over mantels and doorways, particularly at Christmas, are typical of Georgian styles. Fine containers—urns are frequently associated with this period—are simple in design and filled with lovely roses, lilacs, delphiniums, carnations, and snapdragons in a symmetrical pattern, formal in balance and suggestive of quiet elegance.

14. *In this homey Early American setting an ancient burl bowl holds Indian corn,
oats, pumpkins, cranberries and chestnuts. The bowl is placed on a wooden trencher
which still bears the knife marks of the early settlers. A crude salt glaze pitcher contains fragrant herbs including mint, leaves of rose geraniums and costmary (Bible
leaf). A rushlight, placed beside an open Bible, holds bayberry candle. Appointments
tell the story of a rugged and religious era. Arranged by Esther Wheeler. (Photo by
Boutrelle-Sevecke)*

ENGLISH REGENCY CONTAINERS AND FLOWERS

The Regency period, one of sharp accent and strong contrast in colors and ornamentation, takes its name from the Prince Regent (1811-1820) who later became George IV. His taste for the classic in architecture and decoration mirrored the French Directoire. English Regency also employs the symbols of the army and the state—lion's claw, arrows, quivers, Roman fasces, trophies, urns. Like the French Regency, designs were drawn from ancient history and the Far East. Chinese dragons, Egyptian sphinxes, and writhing snakes were combined with the austere Greek and Roman columns, urns, and draperies.

Black and white marble tops for tables and pedestal bases for sculpture and urns were used. The colors and fabrics were similar to those of the French Empire, although more severe. Dark brown accented by yellow and white, and dark red accented by black and white, were usual color schemes. Wallpapers with perspective sketches of draped columns and stairways are often used today to capture the classic feeling of English Regency.

Wedgwood ware with its classic ornamentation was perhaps the most typical china of the period. For containers, jasper ware vases with applied relief in sage green and lilac or any similar classically inspired vase would be right. Reproductions from this period include urns in soapstone, alabaster, brass, and domestic china with gold motifs. Vase baskets and jardinieres were used in a fanciful manner, some having pedestals of caryatids or sphinxes in brass and ormolu, some actually enclosing aviaries. Accessories included classic statuary and busts, the convex mirror and eagle we associate with our Federal period, and ivories, plaques, and reliefs.

Suitable plant material for Regency arrangements might include acacia, bellflowers, carnations, calla lilies, camellias, cyclamen, iris, lupine, lilacs, marigolds, narcissus, pansies, sweet peas, violets, tulips, prince's-feather, and cockscomb.

AMERICAN STYLES

Because the early settlers in America included not only English stock but French, Dutch, and German, true Early American rooms are mixtures of many styles. But the pleasant and homey quality of the Early American period has made it a great favorite in our homes today. The kitchen was the center of family living, and the great open fireplace its dominant feature, as in many modern open-plan homes. Sturdy utensils, such as pewter plates, beakers, wooden bowls and trenchers, replaced the English silver and porcelain. Furniture of native woods was of the simplest design and held the barest necessities. The court cupboard and the wainscot chair, a turned table and perhaps a chest or two made up the furniture for the average home. Sanded floors were on occasion covered with braided rugs.

Early settlers were immediately concerned with plant material. This new land was "filled with flowers of divers kinds and colors," the

15.   *Authentically interpreting a room of 1750, the niche, installed over the fireplace, holds a reproduction, in flowers, of an early Dutch painting using a variety of spring flowers. Arranged by Mrs. F. Palmer Hart. (Photo by Boutrelle-Sevecke)*

trailing arbutus, wild rose, sweet-smelling fern, and strawberries "four times larger than grown in their native land."

Small dooryard gardens contained fruit trees and plants for food. To England went orders for herbs. Some of them available today at nurseries are camomile, rue, chives, spearmint, pot marjoram, sage, and thyme. Blue hyssop, lavender, nepeta, lamb's-ears, and tansy are used for ornament, and for fragrance old English lavender, lemon verbena, orange mint, sweet-scented geraniums, rosemary, and lemon thyme.

Native American wildflowers were used for bouquets, together with geraniums, clove pinks, foxgloves, hollyhocks, sweet William, and gourds brought from the Old World.

EARLY AMERICAN ARRANGEMENTS

The first typical American bouquet was the "tussy-mussy." The old rule for making one was "in the center the flame lily, surrounding it being forget-me-nots, steeplebush, swamp rose, innocence, vervain, and goldenrod. The aromatic leaves are found in the spicebush twig, tansy, and catnip. The whole thing is bound together with a species of bedstraw." Flower decoration should capture the casual, charming, and rugged quality of the early Americans.

For a simple Early American arrangement, try red geraniums in a sugar bucket or iron tripod. An ear of Indian corn would add interest as an accessory. In Plate 13, marigolds and asters are simply arranged in a manner typical of the period. Containers may suggest the Early American era without being authentic antiques. Crude salt-glaze ware, coffee grinders, candle molds, pewter plates and

beakers, cranberry pickers and gourds are among the possibilities. Old flatirons, butter firkins, toasting forks, spice cabinets, pestles, rushlights, Betty lamps, old Bibles, and wooden spoons make homely accessories.

Thanksgiving arrangements traditionally recall the lives and times of the first Americans and are especially at home in Early American settings. Materials that lend authenticity include squash, pumpkin, Indian corn, cranberries, and chestnuts. Early American colors were brilliant, but in the mellowing of antiques the colors seem subdued. They are much like French Provincial colors, and since these two periods were parallel in time and informality the styles may be mixed with success. Yellow, mustard, white, red, crimson, indigo blue, gray-green, and plum are typical. The colonists used wool most frequently, spun, woven, and dyed at home. Today's materials reproduce the softness and beautiful colors of these homespun wools.

EIGHTEENTH-CENTURY COLONIAL OR AMERICAN GEORGIAN

Colonial Williamsburg today offers the best example of mid-eighteenth-century decorating. Here, simplicity, elegance, comfort, and dignity walk hand-in-hand with skillful design and painstaking craftsmanship in re-creations of English Georgian designs. In return for raw materials sent to the Continent, the wealthy colonists received furnishings in the newest fashions—Chippendale cabinets, Waterford chandeliers, Wedgwood pottery, carved and gilt mirrors, porcelains from France, and marble mantels from Italy. But while the models came from England, American craftsmen made copies that were distinctly native.

16. *(Opposite)   Suited to the graceful Williamsburg era, crystal candlesticks, container and fireplace accessories (all authentic pieces) are part of a composition which includes fine textured tulips, freesias and snapdragons. A bit of dark foliage of evergreen leucothoë adds contrast. Arranged by Miss Clara P. Workham. (Photo by Hugelmeyer)*

Social and family life centered around the home. Windows were hung with India-printed cotton in brilliant colors or resist-dyed linen in the summer and Burgundy damask in the winter. Unusual color schemes were favored: pale blue walls with white trim, blue and crimson rooms, mulberry walls and mauve, mustard with gray accents, green woodwork with white plastered walls, and peach-colored woodwork. Yellow was combined with blue. Elaborate Chinese-patterned wallpaper imported from England, Chinese Chippendale furniture in black and gold, and bamboo chairs in black set the dominant note. In homes where the Chinese influence was not so pronounced, Queen Anne, Hepplewhite, and Sheraton furniture was popular.

GEORGIAN WILLIAMSBURG: (left to right) Wing chair; Piecrust table; Chippendale mirror; Governor's Palace lantern; Silver teapot; Wedgwood plaque; Posy holder; Candlestick

ARRANGEMENTS AND CONTAINERS IN THE WILLIAMSBURG MANNER

Accessories included the best examples from English and French potters, pewter, brass, Wistar and Stiegel glass, and silver that was reproduced in America.

The best idea of historically correct and appropriate containers for American Georgian period settings can be found in the Williamsburg collection. English delft "bricks" of soft blue and henna tones or brownish lavender, a brass Monteith punch bowl, blue and white Worcester china bowls and soup tureens, Lowestoft bowls, a delft urn, blue and white Chinese temple jars, and a two-handled Bristol delft vase are included, as well as a Lowestoft jardiniere of Oriental baroque style and jardinieres in Wedgwood creamware and porcelain. For dried winter bouquets, two cups of spiral-turned elm serve as containers and for fruit a silver epergne.

Silver candlesticks, Staffordshire or Chinese figurines, antique hand-carved chess sets, old books bound in tooled leather are among the possibilities that can give life to your ornaments and flowers.

For containers, available today in replica are alabaster, urns, cake baskets, silver resist pitchers, brick tiles, domestic reproductions of antique porcelains, English Wedgwood, Dutch delftware, and French crystal. Utilitarian pieces, such as posset cups, tureens, wine coolers, candle molds, may also be used.

17. *Another contemporary interpretation of Pennsylvania Dutch flower styles contains budding cherry branches, ranunculus and tulips in a Dutch milk pitcher. Tulips were one of the favorite motifs of the Amish. Arranged by Mrs. George D. Oblatt. (Photo by Boutrelle-Sevecke)*

To express the "elegant era" of colonial Virginia, your floral decoration should stress equilibrium. Make your design abundant and luxuriant in fan-shaped, rectangular, or triangular patterns. Add fragrance for its own sake and for authenticity, for we are told that the colonial lady did not hesitate to place a sprig of rosemary in her bouquet.

Suggestions for making dried arrangements in the Williamsburg manner will be found in Chapter V.

Fresh flowers suitable for Williamsburg bouquets are sunflowers, goldenrod, white lilies, white and pink roses, perennial and annual asters, tuberoses, purple amaranthus, prince's-feather, atamasco lily, pansies, sweet rocket, red and white valerian, stock, Queen Anne's lace, button chrysanthemums, Southern magnolia, sprays of wheat, maple leaves, delicate grasses, ferns, pussy willow, redbud, Scotch broom, wistaria, fringe tree, butterfly weed, and white pine.

18. *This Pennsylvania Dutch room contains the dry sink, chair and sampler of the period. The arrangement, although modern in feeling, captures the spirit and color of the style. Umbrella pine forms the line, combined with zinnias, geraniums and goldenrod. Orange and yellow day lilies with red maple leaves could be substituted. To prevent water damage to container (in this case a mortar) line with several layers of aluminum foil. Arranged by Mrs. Henry Hauck, Mrs. Richard Svender and Mrs. R. H. Smedley. (Photo by Zoba)*

PENNSYLVANIA DUTCH (1682-1850)

From the seventeenth-century came a contribution to American architecture, arts, crafts, and decorating that has its roots in European peasant art. Pennsylvania Dutch combines the craftsmanship of the early settlers with the lively design sense and robust color of the German and Swiss.

They were a people handy with the paintbrush as well as the saw, ax, and chisel. With such woods as yellow pine and poplar, they created furniture so colorful and unsophisticatedly charming as to be collector's items today. Pennsylvania Dutch folk-art motifs are frequently used in textile and wallpaper design, sometimes for informal and homey French Provincial rooms.

Hex signs and the mammoth stars were gaily painted on dower chests, trinket boxes, the well-known Gaudy-Dutch earthenware and other pottery, needlework, biblical texts, tinware, enameled glass, and even on ironwork for ornamental hinges and straps. It seemed as though no household utensil escaped this attention. Perhaps the most used symbol was the tulip, which had been a favorite flower in Europe and recalled to the Pennsylvania settlers the colorful gardens of the old-time home. Fuchsias, lilies, carnations, and roses were also used. Birds played an important role in this symbolic vocabulary. There was the peacock respected as a weather prophet and regarded as a symbol of the resurrection of the dead, the turtledove signifying love, the eagle, bird of freedom, and the cock and hen.

Elaborately decorated open dressers were filled with pewter, brass, and copper utensils together with brilliantly glazed sgraffito and slip-decorated redware. One of the first American glass factories was that of "Baron" Stiegel in Lancaster County. This glass often had quilted, diamond, daisy, and reeded patterns, and delicately enameled pieces with flower and bird decorations.

Favorite color combinations were red, scarlet, green, yellow, and a touch of blue; red, blue, yellow, brown, and green; brown, beige, gold, and dark green and yellow and black. Colors were used in a flat primitive manner—that is, primary and secondary colors were usually painted in their full chroma.

EARLY AMERICAN-PENNSYLVANIA DUTCH: *(left to right) Pennsylvania Dutch "Welsh" dresser; Early American chair; Cobbler's bench; Trivet; Pewter bowl; Scales; Candle mold; Pennsylvania Dutch tin coffee pot*

CREATING PENNSYLVANIA DUTCH ARRANGEMENTS

Containers for flowers in a Pennsylvania Dutch setting may be selected from a wide range of antiques, utensils, and reproductions. Miniature wedding chests, wooden mortars, salt boxes, cook pots, jelly molds, large mugs, pewter steins and other pewter pieces, wooden shoes, Pennsylvania Dutch pottery, and rough crocks are possibilities. Breadboards may be used for fruit and vegetable arrangements. If you use wooden pieces, copper or zinc liners are needed. They will then hold water.

Accessories to give the Pennsylvania Dutch atmosphere to your flowers can include framed birth and baptismal certificates, butter molds with the heart motif, pottery birds, decorated rolling pins, iron trivets, and other small household objects made at the early forges, such as toasters, forks, dippers, and waffle irons.

Old World flowers that inspired the Pennsylvania Dutch motifs are tulips, roses, fuchsias, and other brilliant flowers. Insert sprigs of herbs for fragrance. Your arrangements should be equally interesting all around, casual and gay in color.

AMERICAN FEDERAL (1780-1830)

The American Federal period was the result of the gradual withdrawal from the more elaborate Georgian style of Williamsburg, because the Revolutionary War had put a stop to English imports and we were intensely patriotic. This period is notable for the con-tribution of Duncan Phyfe, whose delicate pieces were modeled on Sheraton and Adam. Classic motifs of Directoire and Regency styles—eagles, acanthus, lyre, and Grecian curve—symbolized the young republic.

Fabrics included striped satins, imported chintzes, plush, crewel embroidery, resist-dyed linen, toiles, and calicos. Draperies and upholstery employed the republican motifs with emphasis on crossed lances, sheaves of wheat, and swags. Favorite colors were gray, blue-green, scarlet-red and yellow, and red, white, and blue. Gilt sconces, mirrors, and furniture trim abounded. Bristol and delft blues also were widely used. Empire fruit bowls holding camellias and stock are seen in a typically American Federal setting in Plate 19.

CLASSIC DIGNITY OF FEDERAL ARRANGEMENTS AND CONTAINERS

Lack of native hard porcelain containers for flowers encouraged expensive importations of Lowestoft bowls and garnitures, and French porcelain and Canton china in urns and pedestal shapes. Accessories such as classic figurines, Wedgwood medallions, paperweights, girandole candlesticks, and Sandwich glass lamp bases are right for this era.

A Federal floral decoration should stress classic grace, simplicity, and formal balance. Since Federal is a direct translation of European classical styles and has much in common with American Georgian these periods may be mixed in an arrangement.

Flowers could include some of those grown in the garden at Mount Vernon, such as the Virginia bluebell, peonies, marigolds, roses, daffodils, hyacinths, anemones, carnations,

19. *Camellias and stock in a pair of gilded fruit bowls fit this mantel in an American Federal room. The wallpaper and candlesticks are authentic versions. Arranged by Mrs. Laurie D. Webster. (Photo by Hugelmeyer)*

cornflowers, and lilies, also honesty, gas plant, grape-hyacinth, love-in-a-mist, hollyhock, clove pinks, larkspur, snowdrops, forget-me-not, iris, Canterbury and peach bells, false indigo, tulips, poppies, and violets.

FRENCH INFLUENCE IN AMERICAN DECORATION

With the Louisiana Purchase in 1803, French influence began to make itself felt in American decoration. The French styles blended well with the Spanish motif influence in New Orleans. Spanish inner courts were filled with plants and flowers, and French patios were sweet with the exquisite fragrance of night-blooming jasmine and vetiver. Etagères held the finest French bric-a-brac, patch boxes, and porcelain figures. Imported silks, fine lawns, shimmering satins, fine damasks in subdued colors, magnificent lace, and Aubusson rugs were a part of the scene.

Alabaster, Sèvres porcelain, French crystal, and brûlot bowls are suitable to contain flowers or to ornament them. Accessories may include cupids, ribbons, wineglasses, patch boxes, and birds in honor of James Audubon who wrote *Birds of America* in New Orleans. While the classic Greek influence was still felt, the trend had started to overelaboration in decoration.

GREEK REVIVAL IN AMERICAN DECORATION

Following the War of 1812, American Federal developed in an especially opulent and extravagant manner that deserves special mention, since it has become part of the Southern tradition in decorating and gardening. Charleston, South Carolina, Savannah, and other Southern cities will testify to this rich past.

Natchez, particularly, entered on an era of wealth with its one crop—cotton—which paid for the rich marble mantels, the brocatelles and hangings of silk damask, the rare woods and carpets, the Empire rosewood sofas in the spacious rooms, and the rare and exotic plant material in the gardens.

Greek revival architecture lasted from 1821 until the Civil War. It suited the Southern climate and the ambitions of the planters who had grown increasingly wealthy.

Flowers and blossoms played a large role in decorating and entertaining. For special fetes, servants twined hundreds of yards of camellias and rose garlands over galleries, up staircases, and along hallways. Magnolia boughs and blossoms were used. At one plantation, gardeners cut three thousand gardenias for a wedding.

In addition to silk damasks and French brocatelles, brocades, chintz, muslin, and cottons abounded. Hand-blocked French wallpaper with Greek motifs were used, and walls were painted in beige, white, and celadon green.

FLOWERS AND CONTAINERS FOR ANTE BELLUM SETTINGS

French urns, heavily gilded on rim, handles, and base, and decorated with scenes in polychrome enamel, Sheffield silver pieces, English lusterware, French china and crystal, Dresden vases, decanters, and glass bowls are in character for ante bellum settings, as are accessories of Sheffield silver, French china, hand-wrought iron pieces, and alabaster.

Wax flowers under glass domes were popular decorations in plantation rooms and were modeled on garden and native flowers—yellow jasmine, pansies, roses, gardenias, camellias, and endless others—skillfully executed and massed in vases or French urns.

Plant material should be chosen for delicacy and velvety texture. Louis Philippe roses, azaleas, gardenias, lilies, tuberoses, carnations, violets, and stock are of this type. Southern magnolia foliage and flowers are typical. There should be a feeling of freedom in your bouquet, and the lines should be easy and flowing without a set pattern.

VICTORIAN PERIOD 1835-1900

Victorian styles have long been considered gauche, yet there is a certain sentimental appeal in many of their designs. A late Victorian chair, tufted seat, top-heavy carving and all, with clear colors instead of the typically muddy ones, in a spacious room, creates an unexpectedly lighthearted effect. The Victorians mixed types and styles in their search for novelty. "Too much carving, too large a scale, too great a variety of motifs and patterns, and too much imitation" are the criticisms leveled against this period, but manufacturers of modern Victorian furniture have

retained the charm while improving the proportions.

Victorian fabrics included several new materials, such as horsehair and plush for upholstery, as well as brocades, satins, dark-green and pansy-purple velvet, calico, muslin, mull, and chintzes. Some good patterns of fabrics and paper were based on natural flowers and grasses in bright colors. They are used today in many rooms with furnishings of other periods. Roses lead in wallpapers, combined with lover's bowknots, cupids, and turtledoves.

QUAINTNESS OF VICTORIAN ARRANGEMENTS

An old piece of china filled with mixed garden flowers closely massed and no taller than the height of the container used would express the Victorian style. Our arrangements today are softer than the stiffly executed, poorly proportioned decorations of the time. But a Victorian arrangement under a glass dome or a small nosegay of short-stemmed flowers has nostalgic appeal. Do use one in your Victorian room!

Victorians loved floral decorations the year round. Scarcity of hothouse material for winter decoration was solved by artificial flowers

VICTORIAN: *(left to right) Belter chair (mahogany); Rosewood marble top Belter table with conch shell; Pressed flowers in frame; Lamp; Dried flowers under glass; Staffordshire dog; Parian hand vase*

20. (Above) An elegant alabaster urn filled with mimosa, gerberas, freesias, fragrant yellow roses, eucalyptus and ranunculus with a bird accessory reflect the French influence in American decoration. Arranged by Esther Wheeler. (Photo Boutrelle-Sevecke)

21. (Right) Greek Revival dignity is exemplified by this arrangement of waxed flowers of 1840, still in perfect condition, in a fine porcelain French urn. The glass dome was removed for photography. Courtesy "The Lindens" Natchez, Miss. (Photo Knapp-Lane Studios)

22.   *This mid-Victorian arrangement was made for the drawing room at the Arlington Shrine built in 1842 in Birmingham, Alabama. Against blue-green walls and draperies, a glass-topped French mahogany curio table, lined with gold velvet, holds a trumpet vase with three separate flares at the top, and encrusted flowers at the base. Dahlias (white, yellow, peach, apricot and orange), crotalarias (lavender and rosy-red), fern, celosia, begonia, bergamot, hibiscus seed pods, and roses in shades of pink and peach, are the plant materials. Arranged by Mrs. Howard Nelson. (Photo by Pearce Graves)*

handmade of shells, hair, wax, and dried material. (Directions for drying and waxing fresh flowers and fruits are in Chapter V). The Victorians favored magenta, rose, violet, lavender, purple, yellow, orange, or an all-white bouquet.

Because this period is so close to our own, you may have such Victorian containers and accessories as sea shells, Staffordshire flare vases, Parian hands, and Bristol glass. Still others are Sandwich, Redwood, Bohemian, and pressed glass, ornate alabaster urns and compotes, rose bowls, reed baskets, glass cornucopias, wall pockets, epergnes, metal ewers, and wire plant stands. The latter are still attractive filled with pots of small rubber plants, Boston fern, palm, and geraniums for terraces and picture windows.

Utilitarian pieces offer opportunities for imaginative arrangements when used as containers for flowers. Among them are jewelry boxes, Bible boxes, stove tops, kerosene lamps, celery dishes, scales, cups and saucers, spoon holders, gravy dishes, pitchers, sugar bowls, vegetable dishes, and shaving mugs.

Accessories might include cotton and Paisley shawls, paperweights, daguerreotypes and silhouettes, fans, small parasols, glass slippers and hats, Rogers sculpture groups, plush albums, Staffordshire animals, Royal Doulton figurines, and coral.

Flowers of previous periods can be used, but these are particularly Victorian: salvia, carnations, celosia, dahlias, mignonette, foxglove, sweet William, bleeding heart, fuchsia, love-lies-bleeding, smilax, calycanthus (sweet shrub), plumed grasses, maidenhair fern, eglantine, pansies, forget-me-not, passion flower, salpiglossis, and coleus.

MODERN DESIGN IN AMERICA

Rebellion against Victorian ornamentation resulted in many new styles, including the art nouveau of the early 1900s. Tiffany glass, which was a favorite of the time, is still available today. From this era came simpler and more fundamental forms.

Functionalism was the heart of modern design, new synthetic materials—plastics, aluminum, waterproof wrought iron—and new manufacturing techniques were the catalyst. Early modern design is based on the principle that the suitability of an object to its function creates its own beauty—that out of the material and the purpose served by the object should come the design itself. Thus twentieth-

century Swedish silver, German stainless steel, American pottery and fabrics were fashioned with entirely new concepts of beauty. Those who owned a fine modern Steuben compote, a Swedish silver tray, a piece of modern sculpture designed arrangements to suit them. Dramatic forms with strong lines and bold structure replaced mass detail. Emphasis and contrast of texture resulted.

Modern crystal presents a challenge to arrangers. Treasured for striking lines and liquid shapes, many vases and flasks have narrow mouths. The technique for securing flowers in such containers is shown on page 110.

Led by contemporary painters, primitive

African art became a strong trend in home ornamentation. While they are sometimes used with great style, one must be wary of those distorted grotesque heads around which many arrangements are designed. Nevertheless, the impetus toward primitive art had the happy result of popularizing in America such tropical plant material as strelitzia flowers and leaves, palmettos, and anthuriums.

INFLUENCE OF THE AMERICAN SOUTHWEST

In the American Southwest, because of historic and geographic proximity to the source, Spanish-Indian influences are strong. Elaborate and skillful glazes derived from the Spanish have contributed to the development of native California pottery. Inner courts and patios typical of Spanish homes abound. This emphasis on outdoor living is no longer confined to the Southwest. All over America, terraces and family recreation rooms are made bright and gay with decoration in the informal way that typifies the Southwest. Red, orange, and yellow, and such Mexican color combinations as pink and orange, red and yellow, or black with orange and yellow create the sunny effect.

Bottles turned violet from the desert sun, redwood bowls, burls, glass or ceramic containers, and pieces of rock quartz and miners'

23. *Cypress knee, available at the florists', is given the importance of sculpture in this arrangement of calla lilies and leaves on an Oriental teakwood stand, suitable for a lacquer table placed against a wall. Arranged by Anabel Combs Lasker. (Photo by Gottscho-Schleisner)*

CONTEMPORARY: *(left to right) Wrought iron; Scandinavian group; Southwest door or screen, jolla, driftwood; Oriental teak tables with Chinese figure; Japanese usabata; Floor cushion*

samples are appropriate containers and accessories. Plant material such as dahlias, gladioli, zinnias, pineapples, pears, avocados, peaches may be used in the interiors of these homes and, of course, cacti, succulents, and driftwood. These give the sculptured look for modern compositions.

CONTEMPORARY ARRANGEMENTS ARE SCULPTURAL

As open-plan architecture became a strong trend, with rooms divided more psychologically than physically, bookcases and planting areas replaced walls. Furniture was viewed from all sides; it became three-dimensional. Flowers placed in these dividers must be arranged to look equally handsome from the front, rear, and side.

Modern craftsmen believe in the integrity of materials. Sculptors copy form and texture from such natural objects as pebbles on a beach; architects split their house to follow the slope of the land; cabinetmakers study the grain of the wood. This inherent respect for the material is consistent with the best floral arrangements. Good modern arrangements may be orderly and symmetrical or balanced

asymmetrical, but the over-all pattern or order is never forced on the material. Modern flower designs grow out of the natural curves of a branch or the shape of driftwood or the direction in which the leaves grow.

But decorators say that the sterile look with which modern styles are associated is passing from popularity, and surface enrichment and ornamentation will return. If you have handsomely decorated containers of another era, use them as accent pieces even in a very modern home.

24.   *The trend towards romanticism in ornamenting modern homes is demonstrated in this richly textured arrangement of cycas foliage and sedums in an elaborate compote. The material dries well. Arranged by Mrs. Henry Kirschenbaum, in the home of Mrs. Henry Kirschenbaum. (Photo by Gottscho-Schleisner)*

CONTEMPORARY JAPANESE INFLUENCE

Chinese and Japanese art have had a profound influence on American styles in furniture and flowers.

Japan was the first country to develop floral design into a clearly defined art with exact and precise rules. It seems contradictory when we explore the complexities of their culture to state that the Japanese abhor artificiality. In fact, all the rules are aimed at achieving naturalness. Thus the Japanese home is constructed of unstained wood, and the timbers are simply peeled and polished. The padded rush floor mats are used in their natural color. As a matter of fact, natural wooden fibers and other materials serve as a background and contrast for Japanese paintings, food utensils, and ceramics.

Nature, flower arrangement, and manual art are all components of everyday life in Japan. For example, every Japanese house has in its principal room a "tokonoma," a niche-like recess which is the only place that contains decoration in the Western sense. Across unobstructed space, it becomes the focal point of the room, contriving to make a small area seem larger, and emphasizing the simplicity of the rest of the home. If the family owns a painting or some lovely art object, even a piece of polished stone or wood, it will be found in the tokonoma.

The Japanese doctrine of simplicity is the very essence of serenity. The home is a bridge between nature and man, and walls must open or close at will to let in the outdoors or screen out the atmosphere.

25.   *Atop a television cabinet, this modern arrangement of long-lasting pandanus leaves would be a dramatic focal point. Several leaves, arranged outside the container to create interest, are stitched to the ones inside. Pandanus leaves can live without water. Arranged by Esther Wheeler. (Photo by Boutrelle-Sevecke)*

26. *The ceramic tile pattern of the fireplace is echoed by yew in this oriental arrangement in a bronze container. Arranged by Mrs. Henry Kirschenbaum, in the home of Mrs. Henry Kirschenbaum. (Photo by Gottscho-Schleisner)*

JAPANESE FLOWER ARRANGEMENT

The aim of all Japanese art is to create unity. As befits a nation confined to small houses, the Japanese are masters of scale. Beautiful proportions are typical of their styles in architecture and flower arrangement.

It is entirely possible for one to spend a lifetime mastering the rules and symbolisms of Japanese floral art. One of the most symbolic is that perfection is impossible in nature, so everything must have a flaw. Thus the Japanese craftsman will leave a thumb print on the rim of a perfect bowl; the sculptor will carve an extra finger inconspicuously; and the

Japanese flower arranger will use a broken reed or an imperfect leaf as a symbol of the flaw in man and nature.

The various schools of classical Japanese flower arrangement differ slightly, but the suggestion of time, season, and plant growth, and the principle of asymmetrical triangular composition (which concerns the placement of high, medium, and low structural lines) are common in all schools, as is the emphasis on linear design. Japanese philosophy has given spiritual significance to these three basic lines by naming them heaven (high), man (medium), earth (low).

The original school of classic Japanese flower arrangement is Ikenobo. Plate 78 shows details for making a simple arrangement of this school. The Nageire style retains the natural beauty of plant material and its freedom of line. Yet it is not as popular in Western culture because of its subtlety of balance. There are no hard and fast rules for Nageire except that the material must spring from one point and indicate an asymmetrical triangle. Other than that, each school follows its own taste.

Probably the most satisfying Japanese flower arrangement for the modern home is the Moribana. Moribana means "profuse," and this indicates that the foliage and flowers are used more abundantly. Pictorial beauty is its message, and it attempts to recreate a scene by a lake, the countryside, or a garden. The natural growth of plant material is particularly emphasized as flowers growing below the shrub and the shrub below the tree. It can be developed with flowers alone, in which the flowers indicate the tree branches, shrubs, and flowers. Driftwood is often used to indicate new life springing from an old tree stump or to give an impression of a gnarled old trunk with vegetation growing around it.

ACCESSORIES IN JAPANESE ARRANGEMENTS

Accessories are seldom used in a Japanese flower arrangement as they detract from the linear beauty of the plant. In Moribana water-viewing arrangements, however, a crab or crane can be placed in the water, since this is its natural habitat. But accessories in contemporary room settings may be used to echo the Far Eastern note set by the arrangement. Antique stone heads, Oriental scrolls, teakwood stands, Shoji dividers, delicate fretwork, and traditional lacquer work are all at home in Japanese style rooms.

Flower arrangements are made in "usabatas," bronze containers with platelike tops; "suibans," low pottery bowls and rectangular containers; and "sunibachis," bronze rectangular containers. Neutral colors—the brown of earth, the green of moss and grass, and the gray-blue of the sky—are also in demand. A container may be oval or rectangular for a water-viewing arrangement, round or square for simple Moribana. When a Japanese container has a lining of turquoise blue, you will know that it is to be used for a water-viewing arrangement, the turquoise blue representing water. Today, utilitarian pieces such as the charcoal brazier and the round teapot are also being used for flowers. Stands of bamboo, teak, and burl are both decorative and protective for use under Japanese flower arrangements.

Plant material is almost unlimited in the art of Japanese flower arrangement. The following materials have strong linear patterns: aspidistra, bamboo, cryptomeria, hosta (perennial herbs known as plantain lilies), Japanese holly, iris, juniper, ligustrum, magnolia, Japanese maple, nandina, narcissus, peony, podocarpus, wistaria, and willow.

27.   *For a sectional desk in a modern home, clipped palmetto and the seed pods of cedrus atlantica glauca are designed as part of a wall composition. The plant material is from the florist and dries well. Arranged by Blanche Scarlett Phelps, in the home of Mr. and Mrs. David D. Weitz. (Photo by Lambert Studios)*

Contemporary interpretations of Japanese styles express their effective simplicity (Plates 28–32).

28. *(Above)   Here an old flower chariot holds three branches of curved spruce arranged in an asymmetrical triangle. Three large bronzy yellow chrysanthemums are grouped as the focus of attention. Pine branches and carnations could be substituted for the plant material used. Arranged by Esther Wheeler. (Photo by Boutrelle-Sevecke)*

29. *(Right)   In this Oriental arrangement for a hall table a small hanging is part of the composition. Carefully chosen plant material includes pine, arborvitae, dried celosia and driftwood. All are long lasting. Arranged by Esther Wheeler. (Photo by Boutrelle-Sevecke)*

30.   A Japanese (flowing Nageire) design combines orange umbellatum lilies and arborvitae evergreen with a piece of dried manzanita branch placed in a white container. The hanging scroll suggests the theme, "Over the Cliff". Mechanics: Fill bowl with sand about three-quarters full. Pour a thin layer of melted paraffin on top. While it is still warm put a large pinholder securely in warm wax. Wire a very small pinholder onto manzanita, needles down. Stick the small pinholder onto large one. Next put arborvitae into position, as shown in picture, and then group lilies, all being fastened in large pinholder. Arranged by Audrey Jocelyn. (Photo by W. G. Smith)

CHINESE INFLUENCE IN ARRANGEMENTS

China has played an important part in Oriental flower arranging. It undoubtedly contributed the material form or basis that was later more fully developed. To the Chinese, the careful placing of a beautiful blossom or branch in a vase so that it could be enjoyed by itself in its simplicity brought sufficient

33. (Below) In this broad interpretation of the Chinese style, a water bucket holds an unstudied grouping of Chinese paper white narcissus suggesting that "spring is just around the corner." Arranged by Esther Wheeler. (Photo by Van Ness)

31. (Opposite) Circles within circles made by Scotch broom carefully manipulated into shape, rosy red weigelia and a piece of driftwood in a Japanese sunibachi, make a rhythmic and unusual design. Arranged by Esther Wheeler. (Photo by Hattie Edwards Hewitt)

32. (Above)   A Moribana (water viewing) arrangement suggests the fall season. Castor-bean plant, bronzy chrysanthemums and clippings of arborvitae, about one inch high, were bunched together to cover pinholders. (Parsley would be effective too.) Dark brown pottery container, with a glazed turquoise lining to simulate water, is placed on a bamboo stand. Arranged by Esther Wheeler. (Photo by Boutrelle-Sevecke)

34. *A Chinese incense burner contains casually placed euonymus alatus, tulips and nasturtiums, with the cover of the incense burner used as an accessory to give visual balance. Arrangements of this type can be used in French chinoiserie rooms. Arranged by Anabel Combs Lasker. (Photo by Gottscho-Schleisner)*

satisfaction. However, we have a wealth of Chinese containers to choose from, bronze, pewter, jade, and porcelain. Chinese monochromatic porcelains are a rare aesthetic treat, both in form and color with such fascinating names as imperial yellow, peach-bloom, rose du Barry, clair de lune, sang de boeuf, and mirror black.

While Chinese interiors are of relatively little importance in our country, it is hard to imagine a period or style where a Chinese vase would not find its place.

III

Color and texture can work for you

AT AN EARLY STAGE IN DECORATING, AS IN arranging flowers, you will have to make some decision about color. You may take your scheme from a favorite painting, a well-designed fabric, or a lovely old rug, and if you use the same color proportions, this method may be successful. We say "may" because color changes according to its exposure to light and to other colors. Or perhaps you will call in a decorator. A professional uses a palette with conviction, so the final color harmony is sure to please—the decorator anyway. Even if it pleases you, it is inconvenient to depend on another person's taste for every purchase you contemplate. So the most practical advice a book can give is: Learn about color yourself.

Color is a subject worthy of your time. You can apply color principles to almost anything you do, from buying clothes to decorating, to studying art, and of course to arranging flowers. Many aspects of design seem to be instinctive—balance, for instance—but planning color schemes for our relatively

knowledgeable twentieth-century adult tastes seems to come only with conscious effort.

Based on well-established principles, you can exaggerate the good points of furnishings and minimize the defects, make large rooms seem cosier, small ones larger. You can plan startling combinations or subtle ones, and your home will look as if you knew just what you were doing. Color is one of the most valuable tools you can use, as anyone who has transformed a battleship-gray basement into a sunny spot with some bright yellow paint can testify.

Here's how colors work for you.

FLOWERS CAN UNIFY AND ADD ARCHITECTURAL INTEREST

A planned color harmony can unify a decorating scheme. Imagine, for example, a complementary harmony in a bedroom. Walls are pale pink, bedspread is wine red, and two lamps are green. Yet the room seems incom-

35. (Above left)   Four flower arrangements for a hall table reflect the colors of the changing seasons. "Spring is near" say the forced branches of pink quince (or use forsythia or pussy willow) and yellow daffodils in an Oriental container with carved buddha.

36. (Above right)   The abundance of the summer garden is translated in this monochromatic harmony. Pink snapdragons, red roses, white carnations and a few rubrum lilies and stock, are massed in a silver container.

37. (Below left)   Colors derived from the autumn scene move indoors in this arrangement of yellow Fugi chrysanthemums, and long-needled pine in duplicate brown cloisonné containers. For interest, one container is placed on a teakwood stand.

38. (Below right)   For winter, dried pink torch ginger flowers, placed in a pincup, with aspidistra leaves (both metal and fresh), are long-lasting. All arrangements by Anabel Combs Lasker, in the home of Mrs. Harry Fine. (Photos by Gottscho-Schleisner)

plete. An arrangement of pink through red to dark red carnations or roses against green foliage placed in the most conspicuous spot in the room gives unity and purpose to the color scheme.

A pleasant color combination in a modern split-level home, where areas open off each other—one room painted soft yellow, another a grayed violet, and a third pastel blue—would be to introduce with flowers the colors of the other room. Put lilacs and daffodils in the yellow room, blue hyacinths and yellow roses in the grayed-violet one, and for the blue room, if it is the living room and so the most important one, arrange the most dramatic and largest floral composition, perhaps combining all the colors in a mass display.

For economy in construction, modern homes have few architecturally interesting features. The elaborate carved fireplaces of the eighteenth century, the impressive circular staircases, the built-in china cabinets of earlier eras have been replaced by plain structure, particularly in medium-cost homes. In such homes, decorators now use color to correct form; for this, plant material provides a graceful note, corrects square lines, and softens harsh contours. (While color can conceal dull and uninteresting architecture, the best designs, in houses as well as in arrangements, are those in which the basic structure is good, and color is used to supplement and highlight the form.)

SELECTING COLOR SCHEMES

There is no such thing as an absolutely perfect color scheme. A color combination that is delightful under electric bulbs might look garish and ugly in daylight. East and north rooms need the warmth of sunny yellows, bright reds, and intense oranges; south and west exposures generally require cool colors, not pale blues and greens (which wash out in bright sunlight) but the brighter intensities of blue, violet, and green. So your first consideration in choosing a scheme would be the room in which it is to be used.

Next consider when the room is to be used. A living room used only at night need not be concerned with exposure, since it is the effect of your scheme under electric light that is important, but a kitchen where the sun shines all day will be more comfortable if done in cool blues and greens.

You must consider the kind of home you want. Delicate pinks and blues, which seem right in French period homes (although somewhat too feminine for masculine tastes) do not fit the pines and maples of the Early American style. Brilliant backgrounds intrude on the quiet elegance of Georgian rooms. In the eighteenth century, soft colors were the background for fine woods, and brilliant flowers were an accent only. But if you are creating a Victorian setting, perhaps a nostalgic corner in your own sitting room, you might consider the maroons and dull dark blues, which were typical backgrounds. Given life with vivid flowers, such a room setting has a different and personal look.

Another consideration is to select colors that flatter you and please your family. If you consistently wear oranges and reds, you would not order a purple orchid corsage. Too, a color scheme based on magenta could be disastrous. The tastes of your family are important, too. "Sissy" colors such as pale pink might make your sons unhappy if used in a family room, but you may have such a combination in your own dressing room or bath, giving it a strong pink or another bright color for accent. Finally, remember that every room is a part of a whole picture, so even though you change the colors from room to room, be sure that all are harmonious. This has the added advantage of allowing you to interchange furniture and ornaments as necessary.

If you select soft grayed colors for such large areas as rugs and walls (they are easier to live with than intenser values) a change of slipcovers and a new flower arrangement will bring seasonal refreshment. With fresh and dried flowers and plants available all year, you can have floral accents in any color you want, especially if you take the trouble to plant your garden in the same colors as in your home. Keep in mind, however, that floral material does not allow you to stick rigidly to color scheming. Flowers are living materials that change color according to soil and sun. As flowers pass their prime, they fade out. The list on page 101 will help you with planting possibilities.

There is practically no end to the number of ways you can combine color. A trained eye can pick out a hundred or more variations in one hue, and even small color wheels are divided into sixteen hues, which gives sixteen hundred variations to begin with. But most schemes fall into the classes that are described in this chapter.

MONOCHROME, SOPHISTICATED AND RESTRAINED

Monochromatic harmonies use different values of only one color. It is a sophisticated harmony making this a good choice for city

settings or for infrequently used rooms or passages. As the eye seeks variety, one-hue rooms can be monotonous and hard to live with. Introduce contrast with line, texture, form, and value differences. If you introduce a second hue, you no longer have a monochrome, so match your flower arrangement to the room, or as nearly as possible, since nature adds touches of blues and purples even in red, red roses.

Unusual plant materials can give dynamic impact to a one-hue room. In a room based on a monochromatic harmony of orange, using tints, tones, and shades from light orange to brown, an arrangement of glycerinized magnolia leaves with clivia offers drama of form. Smooth orange lily umbellatum contrasted with rougher textured Southern magnolia branches or crisp colorful copper beech leaves with bronzy chrysanthemums make another choice.

Plate V. features a living room with a pink wall and carpet, rose chairs, and various shades of red accessories, all pulled together by masses of pink carnations. The room is kept from sentimentality by the dark red brown of the woods with black accents. In the blue family—a Directoire living room based on a brilliant Bristol blue—a highlight could be a Bristol glass jar filled with blue delphinium in light and dark values against a gunmetal wall. In a contemporary dining room with chairs covered in bright red fabric against white walls, an arrangement of Paul's Scarlet Climber or Blaze offers one-hue beauty. In each case, monochromatic arrangements intensify the colors in the room and are brilliant focal points.

Monochromes in the blue and violet family are cool, remote, and elegant. One-hue rooms in the red family will be somewhat over-

39.   *Three kinds of lighting are needed in each room: overall lights for general illumination, bright ones for close tasks, and accent lights, as here, to dramatize an important decoration. Dried foliage of the century plant and monstera deliciosa seed pods are combined with the fresh-cut foliage of Kalanchoe beharensis in this magnificent design. The unusual dried plant material is available on order at many florists'. Arranged by Mrs. Yoneo Arai. (Photo by Hugelmeyer)*

powering unless the most intense chroma is used as an accent, the paler tints for larger areas. Remember it takes a lot of weak color to balance a little of the intense color.

ANALOGOUS COLORS FOR MOOD

Analogy (likeness) is based on using neighbors on the color wheel with a common primary base. Many decorators prefer not to use hues that include another primary. The primary need not be in full chroma, you may use light tints and dark tones. At least three hues should be used; for instance, violet-blue, violet, and violet-red, or yellow, green-yellow, and yellow-green. Red-violet, red, and red-orange in full intensity, for instance, are considered garish, yet undeniably this combination is as spectcular as a summer sunset. If used knowledgeably, however, it is an excellent choice for Southwest, Mexican, or Spanish settings. It is best if one color is used for the major area with two others as secondary accents. With analogous colors, you can establish an emotional tone in a room, making it seem quiet or loud, warm or cool.

Analogies occur frequently in nature. In spring, the world seems covered in the yellow-greens of new leaves. In autumn, oranges, reds, and browns predominate. The sea world offers another hue. Blue-scaled fish, their iridescence frequently divided by bands of black, flash through waters that now seem blue, later green. For summer, an arrangement of blue-green, green, and yellow-green foliage with white gladiolus is as cool as a shady glen.

To use analogous colors well, decide on the effect you want. Warm yellows, red, and oranges will be sunny and cheerful. Blues and greens will be cool and delicate. Use only one hue (preferably as accent) in full intensity and pale tints of the other two hues.

CONTRASTING OR COMPLEMENTARY HARMONY

A contrasting or complementary harmony is based on colors that are opposites on the color wheel. Because the eye seeks contrast, complementary color schemes are generally the most stimulating. Blue never seems as blue as when it is used with orange. This is true for red and green and for yellow and violet. If a room is to have unity, one color generally in a pale tint or dark tone must be the dominant one, covering the largest area. Its complement (usually at full chroma) is used in smaller areas. Nature is filled with examples; pansies, a dark tone of purple with a flush of yellow in the center; holly, just a little point of red surrounded by less intense green.

Flower arrangements for complementary rooms may be based also on contrast, or they may be monochromatic. If your flowers pick up colors already in the room, they will help you achieve unity and correct color faults. For example, try an arrangement of blue hydrangeas and apricot gladiolus in a powder-blue container to unify by repetition of color in a room with sofa, carpeting, and draperies in tints and shades of blue. Complementary color harmonies are most satisfying when the intense color is saved for accent, and its complement used in weaker tones in large areas. For a room with dull green walls and carpeting, try a monochromatic arrangement of massed pink and red roses.

If a bowl of yellow nasturtiums does not seem bright yellow, use them on or against a

40. *The eye easily distinguishes between coarse and fine textures and rejects inharmonious combinations. In this rough stone container, cacti native to the southwest have the textural affinity which the eye seeks. Variety is introduced in the forms and sizes of the plant material. This easy-to-care-for arrangement would have decorative interest on a stone garden table or accentuating the corners of a low concrete terrace wall. Arranged by Mrs. Ed Duble. (Photo by Hugelmeyer)*

violet background. An intense color seems more emphatic next to its complement and repeated in small quantities throughout an arrangement. Conversely, to tone down a color that is too brilliant for your design, use it against similar but duller or grayed hues.

SPLIT COMPLEMENT ARRANGEMENTS FOR A BOLD NOTE

A split complement uses one hue with two that adjoin its direct complement on the color wheel; for example, blue-green, red-orange, and red. Split complements are governed by the same principle as direct complements; that is, they are most successfully executed where one color dominates and the other two colors are major and minor accents. As with direct complements, remember not to use all the colors in their fullest chromas or in equal values.

One day, while watering philodendron, we observed that certain leaves had not received much light and had blanched to yellow-green. They were lovely! Next we noted that our metallic begonias had red and red-violet stems and leaves. With mauve chrysanthemums, there was an arrangement bold in design, simple in structure, and employing a split complement. A container was painted gray with just a little red-violet added to the gray, and this color blended beautifully with the begonia leaves in the arrangement. The container was a carved wooden bowl set on a reproduction of a Greek column with the acanthus design and painted gray with a paint having a dull mat finish.

In a room in which blue-violet covers the walls (a deep tone on one wall and a pale tint on the others), with a gray ceiling and a tint of red-violet rug, a pale yellow chair covering and an arrangement of yellow daffodils with forsythia echoing the yellow hue would be dramatic.

Other complementary color combinations are *analogous complementary*, using three adjacent hues with the direct complement of any one of them; *adjacent complement*, three hues that include a basic hue, its direct complement, and either of the split hues; and *near complement*, using two hues, a basic hue, and either of its splits.

PAIRED OR DOUBLE-SPLIT COMPLEMENTS

Hues such as red and red-violet with green and green-yellow will give a brilliant color scheme. Here, too, materials should be picked so that one color dominates and the others are used for transition and accent. Use yellow-green ti leaves with red and red-violet tulips and a grouping of aralia leaves. Or one might use green and yellow-green sansevieria leaves, rex begonia leaves for violet-red, and gladiolus for red.

Double-split complement is a variation of a split complement, giving the decorator six colors to work with.

TRIADS FOR DISTINCTIVE ARRANGEMENTS

The triadic color schemes call for three colors equidistant on the color wheel. Use them unequally for best results; that is, let one hue cover the largest area and the two others be used in subordination. The triadic color scheme is the palette of the great painters. Inspiring examples are Gauguin's brilliant triad of orange-red, green-yellow, and violet-blue; Degas's quantities of yellow-orange in

ARRANGEMENTS WITH GLASS

Crystal is an important medium for reflecting color and light. Used with dark foliage, which absorbs light, there is "something dark, something light, something dull, something bright" which is a good design principle.

41. *This fine glass holding orchid leaves, bells of Ireland and miniature gladiolus, sparkles against the wood-panelled walls of a family den. Arranged by Mrs. Oliver A. Vietor. (Photo by Hugelmeyer)*

42. *(Opposite) In this "fool the eye" composition, two old French glass bells are used, one inverted and placed on top of the other, with a connecting collar made to hold them. The plant material used is a thick curved philodendron stem rising from the center of the wooden base to top of lower bell. Another stem of diminishing size continues through top bell as if connected from below. Mechanics are two pinholders in a small glass container and concealed by small pieces of blue glass. The top bell holds a bit of water. Arranged by Mrs. Irving M. Day. (Photo by Hugel-meyer)*

43. *(Right) A modern crystal bowl holds a circular arrangement of white callas. Transition is effected by the bud, and half-open and fully blown flowers. Large rhododendron leaves have been rolled and fastened on the underside with pins. Mrs. Frederick J. Beecher. (Photo by Beecher)*

the foreground, a background of red-violet in the girl's dancing tights, and a blue-green door; and Raphael with his triangle design and triad of red, yellow, and blue. All of these are brilliant and exciting.

A more restful triad would use tints and tones of green and violet with perhaps a touch of bright orange as an accent. This is a richly beautiful harmony when carefully handled.

PRACTICAL HINTS ON COLOR

1. Massed color has dramatic impact. The trick is to group your dominant flowers at the focal area, then let color move across the design to achieve color balance.

2. Remember that a small spot of brilliant color equals a large area of lighter color and foliage.

3. Use palest blooms and smaller buds at top and sides of an arrangement, the most dramatic flowers at the focal area. The logical focus is the place where major lines cross, as where flowers enter the container. Use color in unequal amounts.

4. A bright color will seem even brighter against its complement.

5. Modern interiors are "color coordinated" or related from room to room. Link the colors with flower arrangements. A yellow living room with gray dining area can be linked with an arrangement of gray-green Funkia (*Hosta fortunei*) leaves on the dining-room table.

6. Go easy on reds, oranges, and yellows in summer, since they are stimulating and warm. Just as accessories, ornaments, curtains, and slip covers add seasonal variety, so flowers can help create coolness or warmth.

7. Allow for distance; the farther the viewing distance, the softer the color of an arrangement.

TEXTURE AND LIGHTING AFFECT COLOR AND FLOWERS

Modern decorators, architects, and landscape designers are specialists in the art of using texture. Such smooth and shiny materials as chromium, nylon, plastic, and thermopane, such rough ones as terrazzo tile, nubby tweed, grass cloth, and brick, adorn many modern interiors. As with color, modern decorators use texture for contrast or for analogy. But in decoration, as in flower arrangement, too much texture defeats itself. Contrasted with plain surfaces, coarse textures are generally appropriate in informal rooms. Such flowers as zinnias, torch lilies, chrysanthemums, sweet William, or marigolds combined with driftwood, possibly in modern rooms, continue a casual mood.

In elaborate formal rooms, smooth, regal flowers are generally most harmonious, such as lilies and roses. However, there are a good many exceptions. For dramatic and forceful periods, such as Regency, texture in boldly executed designs is handsome and completely fitting.

Remember that rough flowers absorb light and seem darker. Smooth flowers reflect light and appear lighter. Heavily textured materials weigh more visually than smooth materials.

The arrangement you plan for a company dinner may be a disappointment if you fail to consider the effects of your lighting on your flower colors. Under pink lights, blue, green, and violet will have a minimum recession. Red will look intensely red under candlelight. Yellow colors seem slightly darker under incandescent light. Snowy white blooms are showy under artificial light. Any color, however seen under a light source rich in the same color will appear more intense.

Light is an important aspect of interior decoration. Indirect lights set into ceiling, panels, walls, corners, and light troughs create moods. Reading lamps for a desk or sewing corner are functional. Lights directed at planting boxes or in wall niches change the colors of the floral materials. Do try different color bulbs and fluorescent light tubes until you get the effects you want. Blue or green tubes will intensify the blues and greens in your flowers; yellow lights will enhance the yellow, reds and browns; pink lights are as flattering to pinks and beiges as they are to skin tones.

COLOR LANGUAGE

Hue names the family to which a color belongs, such as yellow, yellow-green. The terms hue and color are interchangeable in ordinary usage. Each section of a color wheel is a hue.

Primary colors are red, yellow, and blue, equidistant on the color wheel. They are called primary because from them all colors can be made.

Secondary colors are made by mixing equal amounts of primary colors. Orange, green, and violet are secondary colors.

Tertiary colors are made by mixing a primary and a secondary, such as red-orange, yellow-orange, yellow-green, blue-green, blue-violet, and red-violet.

Value is the lightness or darkness of any color, or the presence of white or black or gray. For example, maroon is a dark value of red, or red with black added to it; pink is a light value of red, or red with white added to it. Orange with black added to it will define brown.

Tint is a color to which white has been added.

Shade is a color to which black has been added.

Tone is a color to which gray has been added.

Chroma is the degree of intensity between a strong color and a weak one. For example, at its fullest chroma, red is at its most brilliant, except when placed next to its direct complementary color, when it seems even more chromatic through contrast. In terms of chroma, colors may be defined as either weak, strong or moderate.

Neutrals are black and white, and gray,

which is the result of a mixture of black and white.

Warm colors are advancing colors, such as red, yellow, and orange, and make a room seem more intimate.

Cool colors are receding colors, such as blue-green, blue, and violet. These colors seem to push walls back, so make a small room appear larger. Such flowers as delphinium, lilacs, violets, and hydrangeas will recede in a design and hence are useful for backgrounds. So for a cool summer arrangement, use flowers in fullest chroma at focal area, and duller and paler ones as fillers and backgrounds.

COORDINATING ROOMS AND FLOWERS

PERIODS	SUGGESTED COLORS	FOR THE FLOWER ARRANGEMENT
Victorian Guest Room	Wallpaper with white background and pale blue rose motifs in harmony with Woolturf carpeting in violet. Antique rosewood furniture. Spool beds covered with quilted blue-green Dacron. Dotted Swiss curtains at the windows. Accessories, blue Bristol lamp and a lavender glass collection.	*Plate* 3
Lower Level Playroom	Oak furniture bleached and stained honey color. Walls that are not brick are painted light yellow. Throw rugs, ribbon braided, in yellow, orange, and gray. Furniture upholstered in a bright block print of yellow, yellow-green, and gray. Gray shutters give an illusion of perspective.	*Plate* 56
Contemporary Dining Room	From nature comes this green and brown color scheme. Leaf-green walls (one papered). Matching green carpet and light brown maple furniture are a perfect background for the arrangement of flowers.	*Color Plate XIV*
Regency Living Room	Warm gray walls, dark green and gray figured draperies, green and white striped chairs, dark green sofa, and bright yellow accent.	*Color Plate II*

PERIODS	SUGGESTED COLORS	FOR THE FLOWER ARRANGEMENT
Room in a Week-end Cottage	Dining and living area. One wall of the living area is papered in a scenic paper showing windows opening to blue-green skies with palm trees and the beach beyond. Blue shag cotton carpets, white wrought-iron furniture with blue-green duck upholstery. Yellow and eucalyptus red duck throw pillows and lamps of white and gray. Sandpiper decoys mounted on driftwood bases with yellow ocher shades complete the room.	*Plate* 51
Modern Family Room	Against a modern screen divider in a family room, this dramatic arrangement of tropical material creates a textural unity for a floor covering of straw mats and wall covering in natural coloring. Coffee and end tables modern in design of bird's-eye maple complete the conversational units with bamboo chairs and sectional sofa. A gay tropical print of bamboo, red anthurium, green leaves on a white background drapes the windows and covers the cushions. Lamps made from Tahitian carvings, and Gauguin prints repeat the island motif.	*Plate* 49
Contemporary Kitchen	Creamy white kitchen cupboard, painted terra cotta inside, sets the scene for this vegetable composition. Marbleized rubber tile in beige, with black, white, and terra-cotta veining covers the floor. The walls have brick-printed wallpaper. Cafe table and chairs in black metal with terra-cotta cushions add an accent of color. Crisp white curtains with terra-cotta cotton tiebacks frame the window.	*Plate* 109
Country Den	Tweedy rug of gray violet and blue twist covers the floor. Early American furniture in cherry wood with Provincial print cotton cushions and upholstery in blue, white, and persimmon. Cafe curtains of unbleached muslin with tiebacks of matching Provincial print.	*Plate* 47

PERIODS	SUGGESTED COLORS	FOR THE FLOWER ARRANGEMENT
Children's Room	For "brightness" use yellow! This room has pale yellow walls. Vinyl with a geometric pattern in gray and yellow makes an interesting and utilitarian floor covering. The furniture is maple with multicolored cushions of yellow-green, violet-red, and brilliant blue.	*Plate* 102
Contemporary Living Room *Room*	Light gray-green paint covers the walls of this elegant living room and is in harmony with a tufted carpet of gray-green and brown. Comfortable upholstered pieces are covered with chenille-textured violet-red upholstery fabric. The draperies are of a figured print in green, rose, and brown, and blend with the mahogany tables and clock.	*Plate* 82

IV

Designing flowers for room settings

COLOR IS NOT THE ONLY MEANS OF CREATING beauty with flowers. Plant materials brought indoors contribute to their surroundings not only through color and texture, but through form and pattern. While some people still feel that flowers stuck in a vase are the ultimate in beauty, to a trained eye and knowledgeable observer, design is as necessary in a floral bouquet as in a garden. Just as in a garden you can achieve a casually natural look, so flowers indoors can be arranged with studied simplicity, but plan or design is necessary in either case.

Good designs are based on accepted principles. These are balance, scale, and proportion, contrast, rhythm, and dominance. With these principles in mind, the arranger uses lines, forms, colors, and textures to create orderly beauty.

FORMAL AND INFORMAL BALANCE

Formal or symmetrical balance results when equal objects are used on either side of a central axis, and they are placed at the same distance from the center. This type of balance is conservative, restful, somewhat static and formal.

To test whether your design is symmetrical, draw an imaginary vertical line through the center of your arrangement. Now, if the visual and physical weight and outline to the right of the line equals the visual and physical weight and outline to the left of the line, you will have made a design with formal, symmetrical or equal balance.

Informal balance results when unequal elements are used on either side of a central axis

44. *(Opposite) Accessories can create balance. Hold your hand over the lower left of the picture and see for yourself how much the flowers and bird's nest contribute to this graceful arrangement of tulips, stock, roses, anemones and iris. The center of interest in the design is generally at the intersection of the main lines. When bird's nest and flowers are added a new intersection is created. With a new center of interest, the design appears in balance. Arranged by Mrs. William Bartell. (Photo Boutrelle-Sevecke)*

45.   *In a flow of plant material as consistent as steps which carry you from one level to another, the torch ginger leads the eye to red-orange dahlias at the focal area. Philodendron and ti leaves make the pyramidal design. Arranged by Anabel Combs Lasker. (Photo by Hugelmeyer)*

and at different distances from the center, yet appear balanced on each side of the axis. Just as on a seesaw, the smaller child sits farther away from the middle, so in a flower design, smaller flowers should be farthest from the center. In other words, you achieve balance by giving smaller objects the importance of space.

SCALE AND PROPORTION

Your arrangement must be well scaled and well proportioned. Scale is the size relationship of the individual flowers to each other, to their container, and to the space that the design is to occupy in the room. Proper scaling is partly a matter of transition, so if small and large flowers do not seem in scale, use intermediate sizes too. In compositions that include accessories, try to keep the relative size relationships more or less true to nature. If a collection of animal figurines is used, for example, the horse should be larger than the dog. If an arrangement is meant to occupy a large table, use a large arrangement in a large container; use a slender line arrangement in a narrow space between windows.

Proportion is the size relationship of the design as a unit. Based on classical proportions, flower arrangers say that the proportions of an arrangement should be at least one and one-half times the height of a tall container, starting at the rim of the container, and one and one-half times the width of a wide container. This is not a hard and fast rule, however, just a general guide for new arrangers. The lighter the appearance and color of the flowers, the greater its proportion can be to the container.

RHYTHM, CONTRAST, DOMINANCE

Rhythm makes your design seem alive! Rhythm is motion. In decoration, you repeat color accents all through a room thus creating a rhythmic path over which the eye travels. In arrangements, a repetition of flowers and colors and shapes all through the design carries the eye along. Rhythm is an essential principle in floral designs because it expresses motion and "living growth." To test the rhythm of your design, see if your design pattern leads your eye to the focal point.

Contrast is dynamic! Monotony is dull; variety is the spice of life. In decoration, "some dull, some bright, some dark, some light" is axiomatic. So in an arrangement have contrast —of color (or of a value)—of texture, of form or shape, of line direction. The greater the contrast the more dynamic the force. As a rule, an arrangement that has strong contrasts (rather than soothing repetition) should occupy a focal point in the room.

One element must dominate. A room containing equal amounts of figured draperies, patterned rugs, and floral wallpaper is a hodgepodge. So too, a flower arrangement in which everything is equal is poor. Emphasize one color, form, texture, and size.

46.   *The largest, brightest Emperor tulip is the center of interest in this L design placed where the two lines intersect. Striped cane grass forms the L. Arranged by Esther Wheeler. (Photo by Van Ness)*

CENTER OF INTEREST AND DESIGN FORM

Establish a center of interest. In decorating, the most dramatic feature of the room is the best place for the center of interest, the place where everyone looks first—a fire in winter, your picture window in summer, a colorful sofa. In flower arrangements, the natural center of interest is usually where all the lines in the design meet. At that spot, place your most attractive flower, brightest hue, most attractive forms. All lines in the design as in a room should be drawn to the center of interest.

When selecting a design form, an experienced arranger does not follow a rigid design but suggests it by gracefully flowing lines. Your choice of a form should be dictated by the space that your arrangement is to occupy and the plant material available to you. The most popular basic designs are illustrated in Plates 46 to 54. Others are shown elsewhere in this book.

POINTERS FOR DESIGNING AN ARRANGEMENT

For an easy triangle design in three parts:

1. Start with your longest flower or foliage as the backbone line. Cut another flower two-thirds the length of the first. Cut another flower one-third the length of the first. Impale the tallest flower into the center of the pinholder.

2. Add the second tallest flower directly in back of the tallest branch, and bring it forward slightly to the left.

3. Place the shortest flower directly in front of the tallest flower, and bring it forward slightly to the right.

You now have an outline for a triangular design.

4. Now cut flowers at different lengths and fill in the basic outline. All the stems should appear to be coming from one root.

5. Save your most important flowers for the center of interest. Perhaps they will look best breaking the line between the container and flowers.

6. Distribute colors, sizes, textures, and space. Do not crowd them. Your flowers need room to breathe!

7. Use contrasted forms.

Spiked forms give height: delphinium, gladiolus, larkspur, phlox, lupines, stock, salvia, and veronica.

Round forms give solidity: anemones, cornflowers, asters, carnations, calendulas, cyclamen, celosia, daffodils, daisies, dahlias, freesias, gaillardia, hydrangeas, marigolds, monarda, roses, camellias, violets, and zinnias.

Clustered flowers are fillers: columbine, geraniums, heliotrope, sweet William, and sweet peas.

Trailers add grace: bleeding heart, clematis, eglantine, ivy, love-lies-bleeding, and climbing roses.

Sweetly scented shrubs for large bouquets: calycanthus, lilacs, Persian lilac, clethra, philadelphus, spireas, and weigelas.

Foliage: coleus, cyclamen leaves, all types of funkia, thalictrum, gardenia, and cannas. Also striped and feathery grasses.

A pleasant kitchen setting features the circular design in Plate 47. Arranged by Mrs. Maitland McIntosh. (Photo by Panda)

47. The circle, a tranquil form, is here represented in the apricot Valencia chrysan-themums and handmade pewter jug and plate. English ivy offers contrast of shape.

48. The oval pattern here formed by plant material in two Chinese containers is a variation of the circle, and a pleasant and restful design form. Red dahlias and pomegranates, green euonymus and galax leaves are the plant materials; the stand is in the Chippendale style. In the drawing, the arrangement is shown in a room setting featuring Chippendale pieces. Arranged by Anabel Combs Lasker. (Photo by Boutrelle-Sevecke)

49. The diamond pattern in the fabric, echoed in the shape of the carved figurines, inspired the design of the arrangement of clipped palmettos and anthurium. The drawing shows a room setting featuring the fabric and arrangement. Arranged by Anabel Combs Lasker. (Photo by Gottscho-Schleisner)

50. *Swirling patterns are exciting and interesting. In this arrangement, the material itself—dried Royal Poinciana seed pods found in a Florida trash pile—dictated the form of the arrangement. The drawing illustrates its effective use to soften the rigid lines of a ranch house entrance. Arrangement by Esther Wheeler. (Photo by Ray Jacobs)*

51. (Above) Dramatic as a bird in flight silhouetted against the horizon, the diagonal line is one of movement. As with the bird (study the placement of wings) this form needs an opposing diagonal for stability.

Dried cycas leaves are available at the florists'; curled ends are tied with wire and secured in a pincup placed under the weathered wood, which has been sanded and left unpolished. Arranged by Esther Wheeler. (Photo by Ray Jacobs)

52. (Right) The spiral form of a fastigiated stalk of.asparagus found in a garden patch, combined with two anemone-type peonies, resulted in this dynamic arrangement. A pinholder fastened with paraffin holds plant material in an antique usabata. Arranged by Esther Wheeler. (Photo Boutrelle-Sevecke)

For an evening setting at the pool, the camellias in Plate 53 glow "like angels white in the gardens of the night."

53.   *The undulations of waves rippling at the shore inspired this design form. Camellias with foliage are arranged in a sculptured bronze container which simulates aspidistra leaves. Arranged by Anabel Combs Lasker. (Photo by Gottscho-Schleisner)*

1. *A gourmet cook's kitchen has a charming window-box greenhouse for herbs, with an awning overhead to keep the sun away. (Courtesy American Cyanamid)*

III. (Left)   A massed arrangement of roses, daisies, asters, baby's breath and galax leaves repeats the round forms of the clock and seat and gives colorful contrast to the dark chest. (Courtesy FTD)

II. (Opposite)   Unity is achieved in this traditional setting through the complete suitability of the formal eighteenth century furnishings and the regal flower arrangement, the colors of which are echoed in the color scheme of the room. Fresh green limes and grapes (wired to small sticks and impaled on a pinholder), white camellias (which can be replaced as they wither) and glossy green camellia foliage, and pandanas are used in a classic black porcelain urn. Arranged by George Tolbert. (Courtesy Good Housekeeping)

IV. (Right)   Even a dressing room bath can be a garden room. Water plants thrive alongside the tub; a tiny enclosed court garden extends the vista. (Courtesy American Cyanamid)

v.   In this indoor-outdoor room the roof is permanent but the walls are changeable. Over the terrace go a quartet of transparent Acrylite skywindows, plus a series of shades that glide between the rafters so that light can be modulated at will. Screens make the invisible walls—to be changed, come winter, for panels of clear Acrylite that conspire with the sun to maintain a greenhouse warmth. Decor here reflects the rustic nature of the settings: old barrels cut into chairs, Mexican packing cases turned into planters, butcher blocks on wheeled legs to make a pair of portable buffets, and glowing geraniums massed for color. (Courtesy American Cyanamid)

VI.   *An enclosed porch with a corner potting shed becomes an indoor barbecue room. Bouvardia, trained on wires overhead, breaks the glare of the vinyl roofing. (Courtesy Armstrong Cork Co.)*

VII. *(Left)   From a second story porch—a greenhouse and potting shed. (Courtesy Lord & Burnham)*

VIII. *(Below)   Orchids, contrary to belief, are not difficult to grow under controlled conditions, and the budded plants can be moved readily without disturbing the bloom cycle. Here, with a brilliant flower arrangement of tulips, roses and lilacs, they provide color excitement for a basically monochromatic room. (Courtesy Eden Manufacturing Corp.)*

Color and texture unify these tables. IX. (Right) features paper plates and napkins on the terrace, with a container swathed in pink tissue paper, but the arrangement of real flowers says the hostess cares.

(Below) The hot colors of flowers and print and the informal "Pebble Beach" glass reflect a tropical mood. (Both courtesy Fostoria)

XI. *A wedding anniversary buffet table features a mass of all-white flowers in an arrangement large enough to dominate the plaids and patterns of the fabric. The cloth for the 42" circular table is made from 6 yards of 54" fabric, cut in half, and sewn together in the middle, then folded into quarters, with a circle traced by measuring a 50" radius from the center. Cut and hem. Other ideas: A fragrant camellia in each clear goblet, a rimmed bamboo tray, and a split of champagne for each guest. The goblet with tapered bowl and faceted knob is an authentic reproduction by Fostoria from crystal in the Henry Ford Museum in Dearborn, Michigan. (Courtesy Fostoria)*

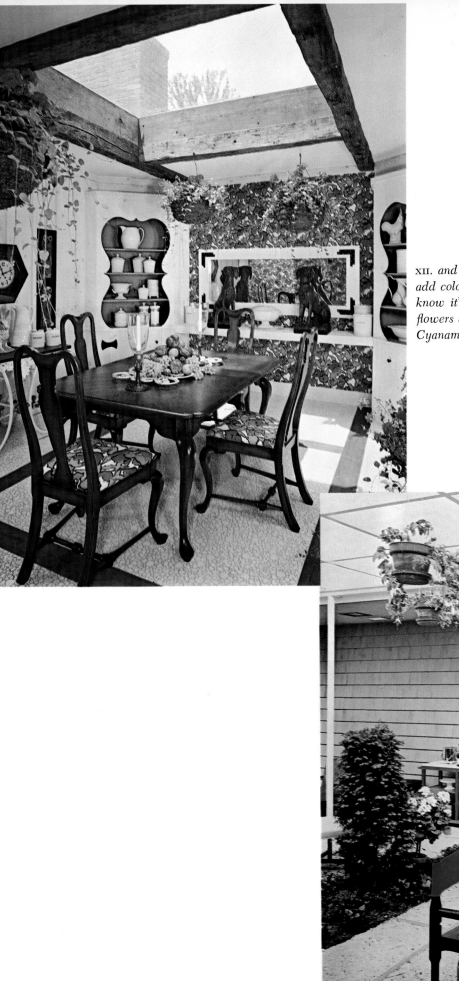

XII. *and* XIII.   *Enclose a porch, top with a skylight, add colorful fabrics or floral prints—and let everyone know it's your garden room by hanging baskets of flowers all over.* [Courtesy Celanese (left); American Cyanamid (below)]

XIV. *Exotic anthuriums and aucuba are arranged with spike foliage that repeats the stripes of the wallpaper . . . a distinctive decorative unit when staged on a wooden board with ceramic accessories to increase the visual weight.*

XV. *For unity, a sideboard design is created in the colors of the background paper. Apples, lemons, grapes and pears are impaled directly into a styrofoam base, held in the container with a cone of chicken wire that extends over the rim. Wired picks threaded through the grape stems hold them in place.* (Courtesy FTD)

XVI. *Holes are bored in a driftwood branch for bromeliads. The other foliage plants—
dracaena, maranta, coccoloba, and ti leaves—with miniature spray orchids in tubes, are
arranged in a container cradled in the branch. Two wise owls complete a long-lasting
garden in a dish. (Courtesy FTD)*

XVII. *The graceful placement of the candles forms the structural line of this arrangement of chrysanthemums, ti leaves (made shiny when polished with milk) sword fern and ivy. Peaches and bananas echo the form, color and texture of the other design elements. The fruit is secured to wooden skewers impaled on saturated florists' foam. (Courtesy FTD)*

54. *Vertical lines, majestic and austere, are suitable for elegant interiors. Delphiniums, asters and grapes are arranged here with great distinction in a Chinese vase. Arranged by Mrs. Daniel J. Mooney.*

FACTORS IN SELECTING CONTAINERS

The container is one part of the design. Because many flower arrangers believe that flowers should be arranged in a manner that simulates natural growth, containers that are earth-colored—terra cotta, sandy beige, neutral gray, or reddish brown—are favorites. However, vases that are delicately decorated with flowers and leaves, when arranged with fresh flowers to match the painted ones, give an effect both lovely and harmonious. And certainly delicate flowers in silver containers make a picture of great elegance.

In planning a container collection (you will always keep adding to it!), be sure to include a low one for use on your dining table or sideboard and a tall one for narrow spaces. Do not confine yourself to plain ceramic pillow vases, flat rectangles, round bowls, or cylinders. Oriental styles have influenced a softer de-

sign trend away from plain geometric forms, and contemporary designers frequently enrich simple surfaces with applied ornament. Although a highly colored ornate vase detracts attention from the flowers, it is possible to arrange the flowers to complement a beautiful vase.

Size, texture, and color are the most important factors in selecting containers for your arrangement. Bold and vivid flowers such as torch ginger are uncomfortable in delicate china, just as violets are not appropriate to massive pieces.

ACCESSORIES CONTRIBUTE TO DESIGN

Well-selected accessories can add a period flavor to your design. Such objects as ash trays, cigarette boxes or lighters, pictures hung on the wall above an arrangement, or books left casually on a table may become accessories to your grouping of flowers. Keeping in mind the principles of design, regroup these objects until their arrangement pleases and satisfies you. Objects should be in scale to each other, harmonious in color, and allowing one unit to dominate. Because flowers usually are most interesting to the observer, you would be wise to make them dominant.

With the help of containers, accessories, and bases you can "stage" your arrangement, carrying out the theme of the room. For example, a sunroom decoration of tropical materials in a basalt lava stone container might include an Aztec figurine in the same material. Birds, Oriental figures, old dolls, antique glass, small silver pieces, and other such collections are some of the themes around which you might build flower designs.

55. *Spiky gladiolus and round strawberry corn are used at the focal point with clusters of Gilbert's celosia, spiraled mare's tail and textured foliage of Kalanchoe beharensis to form the line interest. Plastic foam can hold flowers. Arranged by Mrs. W. H. Barton. (Photo by Gallap-Austin Studios)*

56.   An old iron baking pan (a muffin tin could be used, too) was the unusual container for freesias and tradescantia leaves. Small pinholders in each section held the plant material in place. The base is a slab of flagstone with the same purple coloring found in the freesias. A charming idea for a kitchen. Arranged by Mrs. John Coggeshall. (Photo by Hugelmeyer)

57. *If you love unusual decorative effects, consider this arrangement for a music room. The container is a phonograph record. Cocos palm leaves, dracaena foliage, Jack-in-the-pulpit flowers and dried sea grape leaves, all long-lasting materials, are readily adapted to the sophisticated backgrounds of today's home. Arranged by Anabel Combs Lasker. (Photo by Sam Lasker)*

58. *This graceful line arrangement is tall enough to carry the eye into the picture, thus relating it to the desk below. Had the tip stopped below the frame, the composition would have been less effective, and interest would not have been directed into the painting. Snapdragons, bouvardia, and small dahlias are well scaled to the flowers painted on the container and pen stand, and the design itself is in proportion to the space it occupies. Arranged by Anabel Combs Lasker, in the home of Mrs. Harry Fine. (Photo by Gottscho-Schleisner)*

Accessories can give authenticity to a decorating scheme, lending a sense of living history to your rooms, and pointing up the period flavor of your flower decoration. A hand-carved water dipper or wooden cooky roller carries out an Early American decorating theme and dramatizes an early American arrangement. Use ornaments of this kind as a foil to repeat the texture of your scheme, to continue an imaginary line, to emphasize a focal point, and to create rhythm by repetition. In Plate 73, note how a theme is developed.

59. (Above) A weathered wood form with a camellia at its center stares inquisitively at a haughty bronze crane. Arranged by Anabel Combs Lasker. (Photo by Gottscho-Schleisner)

60. (Left) The original wood sculpture of parrots by Harry Richardson inspired this arrangement of strongly contrasted forms for a man's study. Iris foliage and dark red castor-bean leaves are combined with white hosta lilies and bud clusters in a dark brown ceramic container made by the arranger. Arranged by Mrs. Otto Eisenberg. (Photo by Eisenberg)

61. *Suitable for a low bookcase is this symmetrical composition featuring replicas of museum pieces. Plant material is nut grass seed pods, red canna leaves, blue plum foliage, yellow chrysanthemums and a few artemisia leaves placed in a pincup on an Oriental base of carved cherrywood. Ti leaves with dahlias and clusters of green galax leaves could be substituted. Arranged by Mrs. E. F. Simpson. (Photo by Nadia)*

62.   *This decoration to dramatize an old monk figurine combines cymbidium orchids and Kalanchoe beharensis with a piece of refinished driftwood, such as might be cast up on sea or lake shore. Scenic paper makes a harmonious background. Arranged by Zelda Wyatt Schulke. (Photo by Boutrelle-Sevecke)*

BASES AS PART OF THE COMPOSITION

Finally, most important to design and frequently overlooked are bases, but bases complete the composition. If you have containers that are just right as far as texture, color, or period are concerned, but too small in scale, it is possible to achieve correct proportions by placing them on bases of the needed type or depth. Sometimes a base may be used to complete the line of a composition, as when a flat slab of wood is used with a container placed on it far to one side.

Whether it is a bamboo mat, an Oriental teakwood stand, a piece of rough slate, or a block of some beautiful wood or marble, the base gives a sense of completion and balance to many compositions. It also adds to the dignity of an arrangement, imbuing it with the same aura that surrounds a piece of sculpture placed on a pedestal. A base also serves the practical purpose of protecting furniture from water seepage.

FLORAL DESIGNS FOR EVERY ROOM

Flowers and plants belong in living and dining rooms of course, but in less usual parts of the house they are twice as effective. A few bright flowers on a bathroom counter, in a small vase on a buffet tray, or even in a terrace umbrella, as in Plate 117, has the appeal of the unexpected. Particularly today when our homes are decorated throughout—no catch-all rooms, back halls, dark pantries, or junk-collecting attics—every area can benefit from the pleasing effect of an appropriate arrangement.

How many designs can you put in a room?

As many as look well! In the living room, a bouquet of roses, a potpourri, and flowering branches or greens are interestingly varied. Put your most dramatic arrangement in the most attractive part of the room.

In a room in which everything is in pairs and formally balanced, introduce an asymmetrical flower arrangement in a picture grouping for the sake of variety.

Just as a tall tree on a lawn may be a center of interest, so a large and colorful vertical design can focus attention.

If you cannot afford or cannot locate a handsome original sculpture, try a well-shaped piece of driftwood.

If your arrangement is part of a composition that includes a lamp, use dried materials. Fresh flowers may wilt quickly in the heat of the lamp.

FIREPLACES AND PIANOS ARE DECORATING ASSETS

A fireplace is especially important in decorating because it is usually the dominant feature of a room. The fireplace also offers unique design problems. Relate the mantel to the seating group that often is below it. Plant materials must relate to the texture of modern fireplaces. Roman brick, fieldstone, and other materials must be in harmony with the fixtures of modern fireplace walls and the lines of the fireplace. Stone is echoed in the plant material of sansevieria. Marble mantels are in harmony with creamy roses.

To carry the eye into the focal point, the flow of the design should be toward the center of the mantel, and the plant design move the eye into the center of interest.

63. *This handsome arrangement of Scotch broom which has been gently bent·into shape needs the added height which the Oriental base gives. The base echoes the silhouette of the plant material. It makes a striking outline against the window on a dining room table, as illustrated in the drawing. Arranged by Esther Wheeler. (Photo by Seaf)*

64. *(Below) In this authentic Victorian setting, photographed in the ante-bellum Arlington Shrine in Alabama, Chelsea candlesticks with goat figurines and a Meissen dish were the accessories. A Chippendale mirror with eagle finial hangs over the mantel. The cranberry glass container holds a mixed bouquet of red and white dahlias, fern, rosemary, stachys lanata, and scented geraniums. Arrangement by Mrs. John G. McReynolds. (Photo by Pearce Graves)*

65. *This modern mantel holds a contemporary arrangement of tropical dried material, whose form repeats the mottlings of the marble. Arranged by Mrs. Henry Kirschenbaum, in the home of Mrs. Henry Kirschenbaum. (Photo by Gottscho-Schleisner)*

66.   A pine-paneled mantel in an informal room holds a brass candlestick and a bean-pot filled with gaily colored zinnias. Marigolds may be substituted. Arranged by Olive Allen and Dorothy Jenkins. (Photo by Gottscho-Schleisner)

67.   Distinctively placed on a corner of the piano, this arrangement made in the Hogarth line holds gray-green Atlas pine (its hue matching the wallpaper) and white anemones. A pincup in the black marble urn holds the plant material. The wallpaper is an authentic version of an eighteenth century English design. Arranged by Mrs. Raymond Russ Stoltz. (Photo by Arthur Heitzman)

Pianos are decorating assets but if incorrectly handled may present large surfaces that soak up light. Flowers attract the eye and minimize the bulk. An arrangement for a piano should be grand in scale. Large plant material and containers are required. If you do not own a container that is large enough, make a composition with smaller ones to form an important focus. The polished wood surface is especially attractive for white velvety flowers such as lilies, camellias, and roses.

When an upright piano is placed against a recessed wall or is built into a storage wall, the top of the piano becomes a particularly dramatic stage for an arrangement, especially if illuminated from behind. A large massed line arrangement of garden flowers with fruits is lovely. In a modern room, pieces of driftwood stained and polished to match the furniture, with flowers that harmonize with fabrics and colors, help integrate the piano into the room setting. As spinets are small in size, try small twin designs built around your hobby collection.

ARRANGEMENTS FOR TABLES AND DESKS

An arrangement for a coffee table will be viewed from above. Plant material that has depth, such as lilies, orchids, chrysanthemums, and nasturtiums are particularly good, as is a horizontal design. Since coffee tables are meant for glasses and cigarettes, be sure to design arrangements small enough not to interfere with their useful function. A vivid arrangement on a table in a corner between two couches can brighten a dark area.

A desk is usually a very decided piece of furniture as to period and style. Be sure your arrangement is equally decisive. A well-organized composition is beautifully demonstrated in the desk arrangement shown in Plate 27. The lamp, bowl, and sculpture augment the stylized arrangement of palmettó leaves and a second arrangement of potted plants.

WINDOWS AND DIVIDERS

Bay windows, picture windows, and window walls are dramatic places for flowers and plants because the sunlight enhances their glow, and in any light, flowers silhouetted against a window make interesting patterns.

Room dividers in the open-plan house are often composed of sharp lines that may be softened with living plants and flower arrangements. When the divider takes the form of a storage wall, partly cabinet and partly open shelves, it can be dramatized with built-in lighting panels that will give brilliance to the plants.

To conceal unsightly radiators, extend a shelf along the entire length of the radiator wall. Use it for a line of plants, or have a large plant grouping or container of leaves in front of the radiator. Still another possibility is

68.   *Relate your design to its place in the home. Here twin arrangements of large pittisporum and chrysanthemums follow the diagonal line of the stairway. Arranged by Mrs. W. F. Wanamaker. (Photo by Ralph J. Arlotto)*

to move a planter or tea cart in front of the radiator and keep it filled with a handsome mass of foliage, pot plants and flowers.

FLOWER INTEREST IN HALLS, ENTRANCES, KITCHENS

Flowers and plants offer color, texture, and interesting form for entrance halls when space is limited. A spotlight directed on a planter or table holding a flower arrangement will dramatize it. Wall sconces, lavaboes, and plant brackets add decorative interest without taking up floor space.

Introduce a definite period or decorative theme to the kitchen just as to other rooms. In a country kitchen, scented geraniums or herbs are lovely with textured brick wallpapers, documentary fabrics, and maple or pine cabinets. For the Far East kitchen with split bamboo window shades and polypastex doors, tropical plants are in harmony. For the contemporary kitchen, wrought iron, heavy pottery, and coarse linen are enhanced by large-leafed philodendron.

Arrangements for the kitchen should be simple and wholesome in appearance. Fruits and vegetables are always fitting. In an aqua or turquoise kitchen, a composition of lemons, bananas, and yellow narcissus in a wooden bowl offers sunny contrast to the scheme.

Such pleasing old-fashioned containers as a butter tub filled with flowering tree branches, or grapes in an Early American tiered wooden spoon holder, are clever in the kitchen. A wooden mortar with the pestle tied into the composition, bright enameled casseroles, gourd-shaped vinegar and oil cruets, and beanpots are charming containers. An ap-

pealing sight in the kitchen is a mass of simple flowers of one kind, such as daisies, daffodils, asters, tulips, or chrysanthemums.

FLOWERS FOR BEDROOM AND BATH

There is the appeal of the unexpected in flowers in the bathroom. The combination of steam from the tub and sunlight from the window makes an ideal climate for some plants. Arrange them on top of a large hanging wall cabinet or on an enclosed radiator. A mirror doubles the effect.

Because the bedroom is a place to relax, your eye will linger long on any object of beauty in the room far more than in most other surroundings. A lovely flower arrangement will be fully appreciated here. In Plate 70, for example, Queen Anne's lace in a silver compote gives exquisite grace to the walls of a colonial bedroom. (White walls, too, are an effective foil for flowers.)

To capture an atmosphere of repose and relaxation, use round forms and quiet colors. Avoid spiky forms, elaborate designs, harsh textures, and great contrasts. Motifs in chintzes, quilts, linens can be pleasantly echoed in a design with the actual flowers.

Canopied beds, pavilion bed areas, and French Provincial open-front cupboard beds are old-fashioned favorites that are regaining popularity. A shelf built in at the headboard or along the side for flower arrangements adds to comfort and luxury. The flowers will last longer if they are removed to a cooler spot at night.

For a man's bedroom-study, hydrangea foliage, white bell-shaped funkia flowers placed in a pincup on a burl board are strong and dynamic.

69. *Coarse plant materials are appropriate to the pleasant informality of wood pan-elling. A fiber basket holds picturesque branches of bristling crown of thorns, a reliable house plant with small scarlet flowers, and tropical fruit such as papayas, limes and oranges, in a colorful arrangement for a kitchen or all-purpose room. Arranged by Mrs. Langdon Simons. (Photo by Hugelmeyer)*

For a pale blue and beige bedroom, cover the beds with raspberry silk, and arrange rose tulips and stock with blue lupines and bronze galax leaves in a Venetian glass bowl on the bombe chest or night table.

Flowers give a special welcome, and a guest room is warmer and friendlier with cheerful flowers, a plant or a gay bouquet. The perfect hostess designs with the personality of the guest in mind. Try fresh-cut flowers in her favorite colors for a young girl to tuck in her belt; for a man, sturdier flowers and foliage grouped around a collection of smoking accessories or beside a tempting new novel; for grandfather, an arrangement around a bottle of splendid old brandy and snifter.

YOUR BEST EFFORTS IN CHILDREN'S ROOMS

As a child grows, his room undergoes many changes, but its importance as a place in which he is open to impressions created by good taste and beauty remains constant. Children's rooms deserve lovely plants and your best efforts in flower arranging. Children will be inspired to learn how to make their own with your arrangements as examples.

Visitors to the nursery will be amused by arrangements in baby's honor. These arrangements also make unusual presents. Typical ones are made with children's blocks, night lamps, piggy banks, pastel bottles or jar sets that formerly held cotton, oil, and swabs—all containers for pink and white roses, carnations, and baby's-breath. For older children, the composition might include a night lamp as a background for an arrangement.

Keep decorations high up and out of reach of the toddler, perhaps on pin-up planters and plant troughs placed on the top of cabinets.

For young children, colors should be very bright and gay. Sand pails and watering cans make good containers for large bright flowers. Arrangements that tell a story, such as ones with miniature barns and farmyard animals as accessories, provide food for young imaginations.

Flowers in the window can help disguise a safety measure. If you wish to place a table at a sunny window, but are afraid the child will climb on it, put up a picket fence as a guard, with a plant box wired behind it. The child will then delight in his lovely window garden rather than feel barred.

Make history come alive with an antique Sandwich glass containing flowers on a girl's dressing table. An Early American antique doll, a scale model train, or a collection of glass miniature animals may serve as thematic material and accessories for arrangements. Or arrange flowers around your son's valued piece of quartz or petrified wood, and show him that his hobbies are important to you too. Children will delight in finding field material to be used in dried arrangements that they can keep in their own rooms.

The high school or college student finds pleasure in a fresh arrangement near his desk. Since the teenager's bedroom often serves as the room for entertaining friends, flower arrangements add interest.

REFLECTING HOBBIES IN THE FAMILY ROOM

If the family room is below grade, flowers help overcome any feeling of being deprived of light and air. Flowers and plants may make the family room so attractive that older children will spend more time at home.

70. (*Above*) *This charming little arrangement of Queen Anne's lace in a silver compote could grace a Colonial guest room. How nice with a white crocheted bedspread to echo the floral material and mat! Weeds, those "unloved flowers" await your seeing eye everywhere. Arranged by Mrs. C. C. Thach. (Photo by Laura Smith)*

71. (*Right*) *"Roses red and violets blue" in Victorian cranberry glass make a sweet design for a little girl's room.*

72. (Above)   In this composition for a dining room, forced apple blossoms, carnations and roses in a triangular design are arranged on a sideboard with part of a hobby collection. Cut and etched glass cruets aid balance. Arranged by Anabel Combs Lasker. (Photo by Gottscho-Schleisner)

73. (Opposite)   Ducks are the theme of this peaceful living room in a country vacation home. Even the cattails belong to the marshland setting. Courtesy Garden Club of America. (Photo by Hugelmeyer)

In family rooms, the dining table is important. Since this type of room often revolves around a fireplace and barbecue, dining is likely to be comparatively informal. The dining table is usually surfaced in plastic or durable wood, and accessories and service resemble those used for outdoor and terrace dining.

Family room arrangements can reflect the hobbies of the family. Sporting motifs can be echoed in the flower arrangements, with creels, powder horns, and trophy cups serving as containers. The arrangements can be placed against a background of rackets, ski poles, or other sports equipment. Music rooms can have arrangements with musical themes; nautical ones can use brass and sailor's ropes in the containers, and false portholes can be filled with white and blue flowers. Plate 4 illustrates a family recreation room that provides space for various family hobbies including flower arrangement.

V

Plant crafts and techniques

ANYONE WHO WISHES TO DECORATE WITH flowers must wear two hats—the elegant chapeau of the aesthete-designer and the denim cap of the workman. Many fascinating crafts are involved in the production of worthwhile arrangements: horticulture, so you know how to cut and care for flowers; carpentry, to help you construct stands and adapt supports; painting, for matching containers and flowers; and other useful skills.

BULBS, TUBERS, AND RHIZOMES

If you are making a new garden or remodeling one, plant shrubs and flowers that will suit your design needs both in texture and in color. Every color in the rainbow can be found in nature. If color harmonies for the interior of your home are well selected, your garden will be harmonious too. The lists of flowers and shrubs by color and form and the color illustrations in this book will help you select plant material for your garden.

BULBS

The following bulbs, tubers, and rhizomes are suggested because of their easy culture and fine cutting qualities.

Calla Elliotiana. Deep yellow flowers that are truly magnificent and produced in abundance. The green foliage is spotted white. It is a good garden subject as well as a house plant. All are early blooming.

Daffodils. The following varieties are suggested because of their inherent beauty and excellency for cutting: Mount Hood, pure white; Duke of Windsor, pure white with pale yellow cup; Wodan, canary yellow with large flaring crown of same color. Sweetscented Poetaz Narcissus: Cheerfulness, Orange Prince, and Early Perfection are good examples. All are April blooming.

Iris, bearded. Orchidlike flowers. Examples are Great Lakes, purest of blue; Gudrun, top-notch white; Elsa Sass, a splendid yellow with great carrying power; Chantilly, orchid pink; Casa Morena, rich brown.

Iris sibirica. Perry's Blue and Caesar's Brother, purple, are good examples.

Ismene (Hymenocallis). Also known as the Peruvian daffodil. This is an unusual and fragrant flower with lilylike form, borne in clusters at the top of a bare stout stem. Flowers are white. Blooms in June.

Lily (Lilium). Lily henryi, a rich deep orange-yellow with fine foliage, July blooming; Mid-century hybrid lily Enchantress, nasturtium-red (don't miss this one), July blooming; Regal lily, a popular fragrant flower, white tinged with purple, June blooming; Lily umbellatum, fragrant, orange-red spotted with purple, July blooming.

Scilla hispanica (wood hyacinth). Colors come in white, pink, and lavender and are beautiful in bouquets. May blooming.

Tuberous-rooted begonias. These include many of the most beautiful large flowering types in exquisite colors. When in bloom, the plant resembles a huge bouquet. Flowers, when cut, can be floated in low bowls.

Tulips, Darwin. Tulips come in many beautiful colors, of which these are representative: The Bishop, purple; Clara Butt, pure pink; Treasure Island, primrose yellow. For an unusual and striking tulip for flower arrangement, try The Artist in green and orange. May flowering.

SHRUBS

Abelia grandiflora. A lovely shrub bearing quantities of white and pink arbutuslike flowers from June to frost.

Aronia arbutifolia. A densely branched shrub bearing clustered white flowers in May and attractive bright berries in fall. Excellent cutting material.

Buddleia (summer lilac). Variety Ile de France has spikes of red-violet flowers all summer.

Callicarpa (beauty-berry). These shrubs are grown chiefly for their violet-colored berrylike fruits in the late autumn.

Clerodendron (glory bower). Unusual rosy-red flowers in late August.

Clethra alnifolia rosea. A useful shrub and easy to grow, bearing sweetly scented pink flowers when most needed in late summer.

Enkianthus campanulatus. Bearing pendulous, bell-shaped, yellowish, tinged with red flowers in May and brilliantly colored foliage in the fall.

Euonymus alatus. Has curiously winged stems and brilliant red foliage in the fall. Stems and foliage are excellent for cutting.

Forsythia spectabilis. Large showy golden bells in early April.

Hydrangea hortensis. Flowers in large panicles in late summer, colors ranging from pink to violet to blue.

Kolkwitzia amabilis (Beautybush). A picture of grace and beauty with its long curving branches smothered with pale pink flowers in May.

Lilac (French hybrids). Katherine Havemeyer, flowers large double, cobalt-blue flushed with mauve; President Lincoln, single large florets in Wedgwood blue; Miss Ellen Willmott, double flowers of purest white and fragrant; Ludwig Spaeth, deep purple; Mme. A. Buchner, orchid-pink. All are excellent varieties and bloom in May. Joseika, a Hungarian lilac, blooms in June and is a lovely purple.

Philadelphus virginalis. Fragrant double white flowers in May and September.

Pyracantha. Masses of white flowers followed by many brilliant orange-red berries in the fall.

Rosa hugonis. A splendid rose shrub, with delicate yellow single flowers produced on long arching sprays in early May, and remaining attractive for the rest of the season.

Spiraea vanhouttei. A graceful pendulous shrub that surpasses all other spiraeas. Pure white delicate flowers in late April, and brilliant red foliage in the fall.

Viburnum carlesi. An early flowering shrub with globe-shaped, fragrant, waxy-white flowers. In early May. Its green foliage is handsome.

Viburnum dilatatum. A handsome bush particularly attractive from July to December when its blossoms are replaced by golden yellow fruits. Can be combined wtih gladiolus, dahlias, and chrysanthemums.

Viburnum sieboldi. Lustrous handsome green leaves. Large clustered white flowers followed by berries changing from red to black.

Vitex (chaste tree). Has long spikes of lavender flowers that are fragrant and long-lasting. August-September bloom.

FAVORITE PERENNIALS FOR THE GARDEN

Here is our list of favorite perennials for the garden and for cutting. They are available at most nurseries.

Aconitum napellus. Long three-foot spiked blossoms of dark blue with handsome dark green foliage. September blooming. Beautiful form and color and a blue ribbon winner.

Anemone japonica variety Queen Charlotte. Large waxy semi-double flesh-pink flowers. September-October blooming.

Aster Frikarti. Blue-violet daisylike flowers blooming from June to frost. One of our finest perennials.

Aster Harrington's Pink. A choice outstanding pink aster. September blooming.

Baptisia australis. Three-foot spikes holding lupine-like blue flowers. June blooming. Gray-green foliage excellent for cutting.

Chrysanthemum. Blooming begins in August and continues to frost. Examples are: double, Lavender Lady, the most distinct pure lavender ever offered; button, Little Bob, mahogany bronze; pompon, Butterball, ball-like form, dark lemon-yellow; spoon, orchid-pink; cushion, Major, the finest pink; Korean (daisylike form) Mrs. Pierre S. duPont, golden peach.

Delphinium belladonna. A fine light blue delphinium unsurpassed for cutting. Blooms June to September.

Delphinium chinensis. Feathery foliage. Gentian-blue flowers in panicles. Very free blooming.

Dictamnus (fraxinella). This is a gem and unusual. Flowers come in white and rose. Excellent foliage. Blooms in May.

Echinops (globe thistle). Metallic blue thistle-like flowers blooming from July to October.

Helleborus niger (Christmas rose). Flowers are very large. White with a tinge of purple. Blooms begin in November and last through February.

Hemerocallis (day lilies). Many flowers born on long stalks with lily-shaped blossoms. June to September bloom. All good. Hyperion, finest yellow; Red Sox, excellent red.

Hosta (funkia fortunei). Heavily textured gray-green foliage and waxy white fragrant flowers. Foliage useful for cutting.

Liatris spicata variety September Glory. Has enormous spikes of purplish-rose flowers blooming in late August and September.

Oriental poppy (papaver orientale). Rich in color and distinctive in form. Examples are: Indian Chief, a dramatic red; Barr's White, very exotic with its black center; Helen Elizabeth, a fine pink. June blooming.

Peony (paeonia). Fragrant handsome flowers blooming in May. Good examples are: Chinese double, Mons. Jules Elie, silvery pink; LeCygne, white, perfect form; Mary Brand, an outstanding crimson. Japanese or anemone type, Alstead, deep pink with yellow petaloids; Krinkled White, an exquisite flower, liked crinkled crepe paper. Stems tall, slender, and strong, an excellent subject for cutting. Charm, a dark red with dark red petaloids.

Peony Tree (paeonia moutan). All varieties good, but Bird of Rimpo an outstanding beauty. Rich purple coloring with a small yellow center. May blooming.

Phlox decussata. Examples are Miss Lingard, a good white; Enchantress, a soft pink; D. Comye, a dark red. Many other good colors. Bloom July and August.

Platycodon grandiflorum. Large three-inch blue bell-shaped flowers, easy to grow and prolific when well established. Bloom July and August.

Saxifrage megasea. Leathery leaves, green with a purple cast; flower, lush red-violet, blooming in May. Foliage excellent for cutting nine months of the year.

Thalictrum glaucum (gray-green meadow rue). An elegant perennial with maidenhairlike foliage. Useful in Victorian bouquets. It bears Chinese-yellow fragrant flowers in July.

Thermopsis caroliniana. Long spikes of yellow lupine-like flowers in June. Fine for cutting and in the border.

Trollius ledebouri (globe flower). A magnificent variety of this flower in deep orange, especially good for cutting.

THE BASIC ANNUALS

Mr. Paul Frese has given us permission to include (from his article in *National Gardener*) this condensed list of high-quality standard varieties of annuals recommended for cutting.

Aster Bouquet Powderpuffs. Full-double, quill petalled, three-inch flowers on narrow two-foot plant. Mixed colors only.

Calendula Pacific Beauty. Heat resistant. Large double flowers. In four separate colors (gold, apricot, cream, lemon) and in mixture.

Celosia Golden Fleece. Giant plume type. Two to three feet high. Pure gold. Good for mass planting, cutting and drying.

Cleome Pink Queen. A stately tall plant to four feet high. Ideal for mass display. Continuous blooming all season. Variety *Helen Campbell* is white.

Cosmos Radiance. Five to six feet tall. Deep rose with crimson center band. An airy, graceful plant.

Dahlia Unwin's Hybrid. Extremely colorful, easily grown from seed the first season. Low bushy plants needing no staking. Colors warm or pale, mixed. Three-inch flowers semi-double.

Dianthus Brilliant. Easily grown. Large, plain-edged flowers in rich colors with contrasting eye. Eighteen inches.

Marigold Glitters. Tall, early flowering. Canary-yellow, chrysanthemum flowered. Erect and bush. Three-inch blooms.

Marigold Naughty Marietta. Dwarf single French type. Golden yellow with maroon center. Fine for beds and edging.

Nasturtium Cherry Rose. Dwarf giant double type. Plants one to one and one-half feet high. Not trailing. Flowers cover plant. Fragrant.

Nicotiana Sensation Hybrid. Compact, sturdy plants. Wide color range including wine and chartreuse. Good in part shade. Stays open day and night.

Petunia Carnival. F2 hybrid. Flowers large, ruffled, in mixed colors—pink, red, blue, white, etc. Plants twelve inches high, two feet across.

Petunia Fire Dance. Flowers, large ruffled, salmon-scarlet with yellow throat. Compact foot-high plants.

Petunia White Magic. Large, pure white flowers. Plants compact. Very free-flowering.

Phlox Globe, mixed. Compact, dwarf, ball-shaped plants. In usual phlox colors.

Salvia St. John's Fire. Begins flowering early. Brilliant scarlet. Blooms to frost. Alternate variety, *America.*

Snapdragon Tetra. (Pink shades suggested.) Vigorous plants, large flowers.

Sweet Pea Cuthbertson Floribunda Mixed. Six-foot vines give stems carrying five or more flowers each. Good color range. Very heat resistant.

Verbena Floradale Beauty. Color varies from brilliant rose-pink to deep rose-red. Alternate choice, Sparkle, scarlet red.

Zinnia New Century, mixed. Very large, full-double flowers in mixed pastel colors. Plants branched, two feet.

HOW TO CUT AND CONDITION FLOWERS

1. Cut your flowers with a sharp pair of scissors or pruners (a dull tool injures the plants) either early in the morning or after sundown when the stems are filled with water. Carry a pail of water into the garden into which you can plunge newly cut stems to reduce shock. (The cutting of flowers is good for the plant.) Once indoors, cut about an inch off each flower stem *under water* and place the flowers in a pail of cool water, away from drafts, for several hours. This will prolong their life for a few days.

2. Flowers that have been left out of water for a short time can be revived. Place them in a tall narrow container, and pour boiling water around the stems. Let them stand for a few minutes, then plunge them into cold water. Some flowers and leaves will last longer if they have been completely submerged under water for a few hours. These include lilacs

(remove foliage), hydrangeas, caladiums, and calla lily leaves.

3. Flowering branches require special treatment. Immediately after cutting the branches, remove most of the leaves and lower twigs. Hammer the ends of the stems about an inch or more. This will help them absorb more water. Place branches overnight in a cool dark place, removing some of the foliage from the bottom.

4. The woody stems of such plants as chrysanthemums and peonies should be crushed with a hammer about three inches from the stem end before they are put in water indoors. Chrysanthemums should be broken rather than cut from the plant.

5. For flowers having gummy or milky juices, such as poppies, dahlias, hollyhocks, singe the end of the stem over a flame to seal in the juices. Add some salt to the water in which they are placed.

6. Calla lilies, hyacinths, and water lilies should have water pumped into their stems until it runs out of the flower end. This can be done by simply holding them upside down under a running faucet.

7. Flowers with weak stems, such as tulips, should be wrapped snugly in newspaper and immersed in water up to the flower head overnight. This will make the stems straight.

8. Cut your flowers when they are in different stages of development: bud, half-open, and full-blown. Flowers such as roses and tulips open up fully so rapidly that it is a good idea to hold the blooms closed until you are ready to display them. To keep buds from opening, use any of these methods.

a. Wind a piece of Scotch tape firmly around a bud, or wrap a strip of narrow green florist tape around each one.
b. Brush white of egg into a bud to seal it. This is especially fine for tulips.
c. Drop candle wax into a bud.

9. To remove thorns from roses in a hurry, rub down the stems with sandpaper.

Equip yourself with pinholders, pincups, crushed chicken wire, straight green wire, sprayer, clippers, flower arrangement scissors, and plastic foam.

CONDITIONING AND ARRANGING FLORIST'S FLOWERS

Flowers from the florist should be crisp and firm and delivered long enough in advance so you can make your arrangement early on the day of the party. They need conditioning too,

so recut the stems under water, and soak them up to the neck for several hours at least before arranging them.

If a box of flowers arrives just before or simultaneously with guests, you will want to make a quick arrangement or two with the dozen or so blooms. Here's how.

QUICKIES FROM A FLORIST'S BOX

With a dozen roses and huckleberry foliage, a large pinholder or crushed chicken wire or plastic foam, and an urn-shaped container, you can make this symmetrical triangle in five minutes.

1. *Cut one branch of huckleberry foliage twice the height of the urn. Allow enough extra to go inside of the container. Cut two more branches one and one-half times the height of the urn (allowing extra for the container). Cut any remaining branches in shorter uneven lengths.*
2. *Place pinholder in center of container. If branches and flowers are too short, fill the container with chicken wire after adding the pinholder.*
3. *Stick tallest branch in center of pinholder through the chicken wire. Put curved branches (bend them gently into the shape you want) on left and right, as close to the center of the pinholder as possible. All the flowers and branches should appear to be coming from one place in the pinholder.*
4. *Cut roses in uneven lengths. The buds should be tallest (almost the height of the foliage). The largest prettiest rose or roses should have the shortest stems. Place them at the focal point—where the container meets the plant material. Add water to your container.*

Six gladiolus, stock or snapdragons will make this effective asymmetrical triangle. Fasten a large pinholder to a low dry bowl with plastic or floral clay. Cut the tallest flower twice as high as the bowl is wide. Cut the other five flowers in shorter uneven lengths. Stick the tallest flower in the center and the other ones to left and right. All should seem to come from one place in the pinholder. Cover exposed pinholder with small pieces of wood, rocks, or a few leaves. Even parsley would do the trick! Water.

FORCING BLOOMS FOR INDOOR DECORATION

Pruning flowering shrubs and trees in the early spring can be a happy task if you force the cut branches into bloom early, thereby giving a preview of spring.

For forcing successfully, cut long branches (the longer the better) that bear an abundance of buds. Trim off dead wood, hammer the stems an inch or more for water absorption, and place the branches in a pail of water. Let them stand in room temperature and indirect sunlight for a week or more, and soon you will discover them covered with lovely blooms that will stay fresh for weeks. After the flowers are gone, these same branches can be used again for foliage effects, for many of them will continue to grow, shooting out tender green leaves, so that you will have a new source of background material or foliage for cut flowers.

January is a good month to start pruning. Cutting can be done any time after the first frost, when the day is mild, as frozen branches do not respond. Place the branches in deep buckets filled with lukewarm water in a room with indirect sunlight and a temperature of about 65 degrees. You will find that the swelling of the buds will commence almost at once. Spray the branches with warm water once or twice, or put them under a shower during this period so they do not dry out at the top. A preservative such as Floralife should be put in the water to preserve the life of the flowers.

Below is a list of trees and shrubs that will respond to this simple method of forcing, with approximate forcing time. Nearness to its natural season of bloom lessens the forcing time. If flowers are required for a special day, you can speed up their blooming by putting branches and water under light. Flowers will have less color, however. You can also insure forced branches for a big occasion if you force them successively several days in a row.

FOR CUTTING IN JANUARY

Flowering Shrubs	APPROXIMATE TIME TO BLOOM
Andromeda (Pieris japonica), glossy light green foliage with white pendulant flowers	12 days
Pussy willow (Salix discolor), silvery catkins before foliage	12 days

Shadbush or shadblow (Amelanchier canadensis), white flowers in advance of leaves	12 days
Spicebush (Benzoin aestivale), small yellowish fragrant flowers	12 days
Winter jasmine (Jasminum nudiflorum), yellow flowers before leaves	2 weeks
Winterhazel (Corylopsis), delicately scented yellow flowers in nodding clusters in advance of foliage	5 days

FOR CUTTING IN FEBRUARY OR MARCH

Cydonia (flowering quince), red, orange-scarlet, and white flowers in advance of foliage	24 days
Forsythia (spectabilis), large rich yellow flowers before foliage	10 days
Redbud (cercis), small purplish pink flowers before leaves	4 weeks
Saucer magnolia (Magnolia soulangeana), white, lavender-tinted flowers before foliage	3 weeks
Spiraea vanhouttei, countless white flowers with tiny leaves	3 weeks
Weigelas, foliage followed by bell-shaped flowers ranging from pale pink to dark red	4 weeks

TREES

Fruiting apple, shell-pink flowers	5 weeks
Flowering almond, pale pink flowers	3 weeks
Flowering cherry, pale pink single and double flowers	24 days
Flowering pear, white flowers	24 days
Flowering plum, pink flowers	24 days
Horse chestnut (Aesculus hippocastanum), stunning large, highly varnished sticky buds and chartreuse flowers	6 weeks
Paulownia, stunning large irislike flowers, sweetly scented	4 weeks

Catkins

Balm of Gilead (Populus candicans)	2 weeks
Birch family: alder, birch, and hazelnut	2 weeks

Green, Yellow, and Red Foliage	APPROXIMATE TIME TO BLOOM
Barberry, green and red	2 weeks
Bayberry, green	2 weeks
Beech leaves, green and copper	3 weeks
Japanese maple, red	3 weeks
Larch, gray-green	2 weeks
Privet (California, variety aureo-margi-natum, or Golden privet)	3 weeks
Sumac, dark green	3 weeks
Sycamore or plane tree, green	3 weeks
Tulip tree, yellow-green foliage	3 weeks
Viburnum (prunifolium) chartreuse	3 weeks
Wistaria, green	3 weeks

HOW TO USE AND CONCEAL PINHOLDERS

Your kit for arranging flowers (a strong handled basket will do) should contain sharp scissors or clippers, sharp knife, fine water sprayer, corsage twine, green wire (22-gage for stems and 30-gage for tying), towel, whisk broom (to clean up debris), wooden toothpicks or floral picks, candle for charring stem ends, paraffin, floral clay, assorted types and sizes of pinholders. When selecting a pinholder for a specific design, use one heavy enough to hold the arrangement, with pin points close together. Have a special place in the house for your flowers, with shelves for containers, water, and tools, and a tape measure if you don't trust your eye.

When pinholders are not heavy enough, attach the holder to the dry container with floral clay, or pour just enough melted paraffin into the container to keep the pinholder in place. Use only enough paraffin so that it will not get to the needles. To add additional weight to the pinholder, impale a smaller pinholder onto the first by turning its needle points upside down. To conceal holders, cover them with weathered wood, stones, pebbles, or even glass slags that harmonize with the flowers and container. Glass slag comes in clear or colored glass and can be obtained at flower arrangers' shops.

If the container is too tall for the flower stems, shorten it by using dry sand and placing the pinholder on the sand. Or crush newspaper, and pack it tightly into the bottom of the container in place of sand. Pour melted paraffin on top of the paper, and place the pinholder on the paper. A bunch of twigs from a privet hedge, sheared of all foliage and tied at top and bottom, is also good for altering the interior dimensions of a tall container, since it will hold fine-stemmed flowers nicely.

Glass containers, especially transparent ones, do not always permit the use of pinholders. You can tie the stems of your arrangement at the bottom and near the rim; cover with gladiolus or iris leaf fastened to it or a sprig of ivy. If a pinholder is needed, cover it with a large leaf, and impale the stems through the leaf, or place an interesting leaf in front of it. Fill with water to the top of a glass container to avoid a dividing line.

When a flower is too thin to be stuck into the pinholder, tie it to another two-inch stem with wire or thread. Reinforce the hollow stems of callas and amaryllis by inserting a toothpick or floral pick to keep them upright, or run 22-gage wire up to the flower head to control direction. For narrow leaves, such as iris and gladiolus, which are difficult to impale on a pinholder, cut off about an inch of leaf, fold it over the bottom end of the leaf, and impale it on the pinholder. The leaf will hold firmly.

Small-stemmed flowers, such as wild flowers, may be impaled on a pinholder at any angle if you first insert their stems into a large stem of soft plant material, such as gladiolus. Flowers can be made to last out of water. Insert them into a grape to retain moisture.

74.   *A pewter mug holds leaves, wheat, small chrysanthemum buds and dahlias in colors carefully graduated to create balance. The weight of the lid is offset by the greater intensity of color on the left side. Technique for making the arrangement follows. Arranged by Anabel Combs Lasker. (Photo Gottscho-Schleisner)*

1.   *Fill pewter mug with strips of paper or sand. Pour melted wax over paper, not more than ¼ inch deep. In a few minutes, center the pinholder in wax which has begun to harden.*

2.   *Impale leaves, wheat and small chrysanthemum buds in the holder. All should appear to come from the center of the pinholder.*

3.   *Add more chrysanthemums and small dahlias, working toward the center. Leave a space for the center of interest. The completed arrangement shows the placement of the larger dahlias toward the center, completing the massed effect.*

Fill the vase to the neck with water. Place a wad of water repellent clay in the opening to act as a holder for the flowers. Insert stems through the clay into the water, allowing them to just touch the water. Impale orchid leaves into clay on each side of the orchids. Add philodendron leaf in front to hide the neck of the bottle and the clay, as shown in finished arrangement.

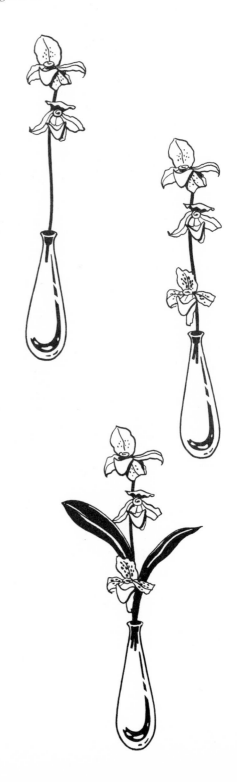

75.   *Transparent crystal presents a challenge to arrangers because the design must be carried out under the water line. This sophisticated arrangement of orchids (now you know what to do with your left-over corsage!), orchid foliage, and one leaf of philodendron selloum is one answer. The drawings show how-to-do it. Arranged by Anabel Combs Lasker. (Photo by Gottscho-Schleisner)*

To float large flowers, such as dahlias, hibiscus, and water lilies, make a tripod of toothpicks, sticking the narrow part of the tripod into the flower, leaving enough of the flower stem so that it will reach water, and place it in a low container.

If a forked holder will not hold in a metal container because of its smooth sides, place a narrow band of waterproof adhesive tape inside the opening where the fork is to go.

Stick the stem of a flower into the pinholder in an upright position to fasten it securely. Then tip the stem to its proper angle. If the stem is a woody one, cut it on a slant to make the branch go into the holder more easily. Hold tall stems and foliage in place by fastening them to the back of the vase with Scotch tape or floral clay, but be sure tape or clay does not show.

FINISHING YOUR ARRANGEMENT AND CURVING BRANCHES

When trimming your arrangement, cut the stems on the oblique so that the cut section is to the back. If it still shows, smear the cut end with cigar ashes, wet soil, or green chalk.

To curve branches to the shape you want, gently manipulate them between the thumb and index finger of your right and left hand, bending them firmly in the direction you want them to take. Do not try to bend water-logged branches. Pussy willow and Scotch broom are more easily bent when on the dry side.

Here are the final steps.

1. Fill the container with water.

2. Remove any floating pieces of plant material.

3. Conceal any mechanics that show.

4. Apply a fine spray of water to the flowers. This is as refreshing to them as dew.

76.   *A long-lasting arrangement in a dynamic spiral design uses a piece of weathered wood and dried artichoke blossoms. The wood can be nailed to a heavy piece of wood that rested in the bottom of the container. Arranged by Mrs. Dunham Higgins. (Photo by Hugelmeyer)*

5. Add water as needed to keep the container filled.

6. Use a stand, burl, or block to protect fine furniture from water seepage.

77. *This Japanese arrangement is an adaptation of the Ikenobo school, using five branches of yew in a forked branch or pinholder. The container is an ancient usabata. Arranged by Esther Wheeler. (Photo by Ray Jacobs Studio)*

FRUIT AND LOW MASSED ARRANGEMENTS

Grapes, lady apples, nuts, peppers, or limes (material without stems) may be made suitable for a pinholder by attaching the fruit to a thin stick with wire, and inserting the other end of the stick in the pinholder.

To hold fruit in place, you can also first impale a potato on the pinholder. Insert one end of a floral pick into the potato, the other end into the fruit. The potato should be com-

78.   Here is the technique for making the Japanese arrangement in Plate 77. Branches
of yew are shown impaled on a pinholder. (For a more authentic arrangement the forked
holder in the foreground could be substituted). Driftwood and Japanese-type knife and
shears are illustrated in the foreground. Rocks to fit over the holder are shown at the left.
Arranged by Esther Wheeler. (Photo by Ray Jacobs)

pletely covered by fruit. You can also impale flowers on a potato when you do not want to use water.

Fruit arrangements can be enhanced by making rosettes of leaves. Take seven ivy or galax leaves, folding the first three upright and wiring them to each other. Swirl the rest of the leaves around them. The waxing of

fresh fruit to retain its freshness is discussed on page 124.

Use chicken wire to secure plant materials in the container when making low massed arrangements. Crumple 1½- or 2-inch-gage chicken wire firmly into the container in sufficient quantity to secure the flowers at any angle.

Step-by-step method for arranging fruit and foliage on a tray, illustrated in Plate 109.

1. *Fill a pincup or a tuna-fish can holding a pinholder with water. Place it at the back of the tray. Hide pinholder with a large leaf. Curl two dracaena leaves around your finger. Impale on pinholder through leaf.*
2. *Place 2 large aralia leaves in front of dracaena.*
3. *Impale pineapple on pinholder; first trim the top if necessary to follow the design. Place pear, artichoke, crabapple and 2 bananas as shown.*
4. *Halve a cantaloupe, remove seeds, place it on its side in front of pineapple.*
5. *Use wired floral pick to support grapes. Wire one end to grape stem, then impale pick into pincup, allowing grapes to cascade over melon. Complete arrangement by adding another pear as shown in Plate 109.*

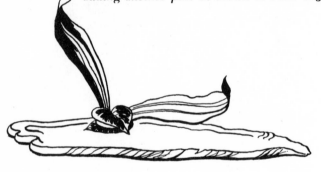

79.   *A handsome baroque bronze and crystal French epergne holds vining ivy foliage to outline the delicate pattern of the roses. Rhythm is achieved by roses graduated from small to large, from light to dark pink. The flowers are impaled on a pinholder in a pincup. The technique for making arrangements in epergnes is shown on the attached drawings. Arranged by Anabel Combs Lasker. (Photo by Gottscho-Schleisner)*

To arrange roses on the epergne, place a pincup with water on a leaf on the glass tiers. The leaf keeps the cup from sliding. Hide the pinholder by placing another leaf over it. Place sprays of ivy as shown in drawing, having the one on top cascade down to meet the spray coming up from the lowest tier. Put another spray of foliage in the lower pincup, bent over as shown in the drawing at the left. Place the roses in the pincups to follow the basic outline of the foliage as shown on the right. Repeat the procedure on the reverse side.

80. *This dried composition used against a screen in a contemporary home "blooms" all year. A pincup on a redwood burl holds pencil cattails, tan teasels, white desert candle stalk, light brown celosia and magnolia seed pods. Arranged by Mrs. John M. Langenberger.*

SUPPORTING DRIFTWOOD AND OTHER HEAVY MATERIALS

Driftwood and other heavy materials frequently call for more support than even a large pinholder can give. In these cases, nail the driftwood to a heavier piece of wood that will fit into your container. Or balance the driftwood in a coffee can into which melted paraffin is poured until half full. Hold the driftwood in position while the wax is hardening. When hard, remove from the can by trimming the rim with a can opener.

LONG-LASTING OR DRIED ARRANGEMENTS

Long-lasting or dried arrangements play a special part in home decorating because they are available in all seasons and all weathers. Techniques of drying, pressing, and skeletonizing can be applied to many materials, so it is possible to have arrangements that are charming enough for the daintiest rooms and appropriate in the most elegant homes as the illustrations throughout this book demonstrate. Dried materials with the sculptured look of carved wood are adaptable to

81.   *The small panel at the left uses a piece of driftwood, two sea urchins and two lion's paw shells, sewed onto a piece of grass cloth wallpaper which was first stiffened with cardboard. Small holes had been drilled in the driftwood so the thread could go through. The center panel, which is about 3 feet high, holds many types of seed pods and glycerinized mahonia foliage. A small guitar, horn, and trumpet, bought at the five and ten, were gilded and attached with wire. These give added interest and make the panel particularly appropriate in a music room. The panel at the right uses dried sea grape leaves with stems, wired to a cardboard-lined grass cloth wallpaper. Arranged by Esther Wheeler. (Photo by Gottscho-Schleisner)*

82. (Opposite) These glossy glycerinized leaves of the southern magnolia, treated several years ago, are still fresh. With orange clivia and the fruit of the baobab tree for an accessory, they make a distinctive monochromatic harmony. Arranged by Esther Wheeler. (Photo by Boutrelle-Sevecke)

83. (Above) "Loved flowers need not fade" if you preserve them carefully. This series of dried seed and flower panels would be a joy in any home. Courtesy Garden Club of America. (Photo by Hugelmeyer)

contemporary as well as Early American rooms, since both often have a textured appearance.

Dried arrangements are particularly valuable as accessories, since they may be painted or sprayed to harmonize with your furniture or gilded to contribute a note of elegance. To paint dried flowers or foliage, spray them with a commercial paint that can be bought at your florist or paint store. It comes in a wide variety of colors.

Pressed flower plaques and arrangements mounted on mats or placed in shadow boxes to serve as wall decorations and collages are among the several ways of using long-lasting garden products. To insure a wintertime supply of ornamental grasses and flowers, you can preserve your summertime surplus by simple and easy methods.

PRESERVING BY HANGING UPSIDE DOWN

The following flowers will retain their color if cut before they are completely open and stripped of their foliage to prevent continued growth. Tie them in small loose bunches, and hang them upside down in a dark dry room. Pick only the most perfect specimens for your collection. Dry spiked forms for height, round forms for solidity.

SPIKED FORMS REQUIRING HANGING

Garden Flowers
Spring
  Larkspur (pink and lavender)

Summer
  Bells of Ireland (green)
  Calla lilies. Stuff with tissue.
  Celosia, or cockscomb (red, yellow, and orange)
  Prince's-feather (red and gold)
  Salvia farinacea (blue)
  Statice (many colors)
  Yarrow, garden variety (gold)

Wild Flowers
Spring
  Cattails (brown). Immerse heads in shellac to prevent opening.

Spring to fall
  Goldenrod (yellow)
  Joe-pye weed (lavender)
  Vervain (deep blue)

ROUND FORMS REQUIRING HANGING

Garden Flowers
Summer
  Acroclinium (white)
  Ageratum (blue and gold)
  Globe amaranth (orange and magenta)
  Globe thistle (blue)
  Honesty (pearly white)
  Monarda (red)
  Strawflowers (yellow, orange, purple, rose)

Wild Flowers
  Pearly everlasting (white)
  Queen Anne's lace (white)
  Red clover
  Sumac (red)
  Tansy (yellow buttonlike clusters)
  Yarrow (white) .

Fillers or Background Materials
Baby's-breath (white). Hang upside down.
Ferns: Will retain their green color if cut in June and dried between sheets of newspaper.
Scotch broom (green). Bend into desired shape, and dry upright.
Pussy willow (gray). Cut when catkins are coming out, bend into desired shape, and dry upright.

84. *A piece of masonite, painted soft blue, is the background for this picture. The frame is wood molding, painted white then rubbed with a little gray. Hay-scented fern (dried a soft green) is the line, and apricot stock with chartreuse green top buds, and blue, yellow and purple pansies are the other plant materials. Two quizzical penguins complete a charming composition.*

To dry flowers: *Pour two inches of builder's sand in a pan or box. Lay the flowers in it (pansies upside down with stems sticking up), one layer deep. Sprinkle more sand gently on the flowers until they are barely covered. Place in a warm place, on radiator or top of furnace, until thoroughly dried, in about a week or so. Treat a few more than needed so that there will be some spares, and a few to look at to determine when they are ready to be taken from sand. Remove very gently. Be careful when gluing them to background as they are brittle.*

A gentle steaming with a kettle every six months will refresh the picture. This one is still bright and colorful after three years. Arranged by Mrs. J. H. M. Wilson. (Photo by Panda)

PRESERVING WITH BORAX

The following flowers require a borax and sand treatment. Add one cup of borax to two cups of builder's sand. Place this mixture, thoroughly stirred, in a low container or shoe box. Place the flowers in the boxes heads down and thoroughly covered with sand. Leave stems exposed and upright. In about two weeks, when the stems are dry to the touch, remove the flowers from the mixture.

SPIKED FORMS REQUIRING BORAX

Garden Flowers

Spring
  Delphinium (blue to violet)
  Lilacs (pink to lavender to blue)
  Spiraea vanhouttei (white)

ROUND FORMS REQUIRING BORAX

Summer
  Carnations (many colors)
  Dahlias, small type (many colors)
  Hydrangeas (blue, pink, and metallic green)
  Marigolds (yellow and brown)
  Peonies (pink and red preferred)
  Platycodon (blue)
  Shasta daisies (white)
  Zinnias (coral, pink, and yellow preferred)

DRIED SEEDHEADS AND ORNAMENTAL GRASSES

Seedheads are frequently used in plaques and arrangements of dried materials. Cut them when green (before they open), and place them in a dry room.

Garden Flowers

  Baptisia australis (black)
  Iris siberian (brown)
  Peony (brown)

  Poppy (brown)
  Rose hips (scarlet)
  Thermopsis (tan)
  Tulips (tan)

Wild Flowers

  Bayberry (gray)
  Milkweed (tan)
  Mullein (gray-green)

Ornamental grasses are good as background materials. Gather them before they go to seed, and place them upright in a jar to dry.

  Bamboo (gray)
  Barley and broom corn (beige)
  Cloud grass (tufted)
  Fountain and pampas grass (tufted)
  Job's-tears (dried flower panicles)
  Millet (dark brown)
  Natal grass (reddish flowers)
  Oats and rye (beige)
  Sorghum (beige to brown)
  Timothy (green)

PRESERVING FOLIAGE WITH GLYCERINE

A method of preserving material that is almost exclusively used for foliage is the glycerine method. Glycerine gives a most lasting life to leaves and also a smooth satinlike gloss. Some leaves change color with this method: barberry, for example, when treated in the spring turns bright red in glycerine, although if treated in the fall it turns brown. Some leaves turn bright yellow if left in the solution long enough, and an interesting mottled effect can be obtained according to the type of material and the length of time it is left in the solution.

To glycerinize leaves, cut the foliage after a dry spell (or there will be no induction of the solution), removing all damaged leaves. Pound the stems to split them. Place the stems upright in a jar containing four ounces of glycerine to sixteen ounces of water. This amount will take care of enough stems for a large bouquet. Add water to the glycerine as it evaporates. There is no need to add more glycerine. (After the commercial "Prestone" solution has winterized your car, save the remains. It will serve the same purpose and take care of more foliage.) It will take two to five weeks for stems and foliage to absorb the solution. When you can feel the glycerine on the outer edges of the leaves, the branches can be removed and stored in boxes until needed. The leaves will remain soft and pliable for years.

The following plant materials lend themselves easily to glycerinizing, and you may preserve them whenever foliage is available.

Autumn oak
Barberry
Beech
Canna leaves
Copper beech
Dogwood
Eucalyptus
Flowering plum
Loquat
Mahonia or Oregon holly
Maple
Rhododendron
Southern magnolia
Viburnum sieboldi

SKELETONIZING LEAVES

Another treatment for foliage, effective in long-lasting arrangements, is skeletonizing. Leaves that may be skeletonized are maple, oak, Southern magnolia, loquat, or any heavy-textured leaf. Strip the leaves one at a time from the stem, and place them in a solution of one tablespoon of sal soda for each quart of water. Boil them for at least one-half hour, allowing them to cool in the solution.

Now run cool water over the leaves, and place them on a wooden board. Gently remove the fleshy part of each leaf with a nylon handbrush until only the skeleton is left. Then place the skeletonized leaves in a solution of two tablespoons of Clorox mixed with one quart of water, and allow them to remain for an hour and fifteen minutes.

Remove the leaves, and place them in a bath of cold water. You may tint them pastel shades of green, pink, or yellow. Wipe them carefully and place them between sheets of absorbent paper, carefully reshaping the leaf forms. Press them between heavy weights.

EXOTIC MATERIALS

Your florist can supply many of the following unusual plants or can order them for you. If you get them fresh, use them, but do not replenish their water supply. They will gradually dry and can be used for a long time for dramatic effects.

SEED PODS

Allamanda pods (elongated shapes, beige)
Baobab pods (shaped like large tulips, brown)
Coconut blossom stems (fine stems with decoration, beige)
Cotton blossoms (star-shaped, brown)
Date palm (heavily textured, brown, bell-shaped)
Elephant's ear (shaped like an ear, black)
Eucalyptus (some twelve varieties, interesting shapes, brown and black)
Hawaiian "wooden roses" (beautifully shaped "roses," tan and brown)
Jacaranda (flat disk-shaped pods, beige)
Lotus (interesting round forms with perforations, black and brown)
Pomegranate (shaped like an apple, grayed-rose)
Royal Poinciana (swordlike form with curious decorations inside pod, brown)
St.-John's-bread (form resembles pea pods, brown)
Sterculia (heart-shaped, brown)

Traveler's-tree (clustered bunches with cottony blue
seeds)
Yucca (clusters of elongated forms, beige to brown)

FOLIAGE

Bird of paradise (heavily textured, gray-green). Put
in a dry place.
Climbing milkweed (curiously twisted forms, gray-
green)
Coconut palm spathes (tan and brown). Put in a dry
place.
Cycas (leathery foliage, tan). Bend into shape before
drying.
Fiddle leaf (heavily textured with ribbing, gray-
green)
Leucadendron, silver tree (elongated small leaves,
silvery gray)
Lotus (rounded fragile leaves, dark green)
Orchid foliage (very heavily textured, green and
brown)
Palmettos (gray-green, interesting when clipped)
Rubber plant (heavily textured, strong rib, tan)
Sea grape leaves (round, medium size, heavily tex-
tured, copper red)
Southern magnolia (medium-sized leaf, tan)

FRUITS AND VEGETABLES, DRIED OR WAXED

Oranges, lemons, limes, pineapples, avocados,
artichokes, mangoes, and pomegranates can
be easily dried. Merely lay them on a flat surface in a very dry place (in your attic or on
top of the basement furnace or in a closet)
until firm. Hardening usually begins within a
week after the fruit has passed through a pre-
liminary soft stage.

Waxed fruit and vegetable arrangements
are most attractive, their colors having a
pearly translucence, and they are most appropriate for the Victorian period. Use fresh
fruit that is hard to the touch. It should be
wiped dry.

To wax, impale each fruit on a large toothpick, or run a wire loop through it, especially
if you are waxing grapes. Then place three
blocks of paraffin in a tin coffee can that has
been placed in a larger pan of water (to prevent fire hazard), and set it over a slow flame.
When the wax is almost melted, add one white
crayon. This will give an opaque effect to
your material. When the wax is thoroughly
melted, remove it from the flame, and cool it
slightly. Dip the fruits and vegetables quickly
into this solution. The result should be a very
fine film suggestive of alabaster over the entire piece.

The material is now ready to be arranged
in your container. If necessary, use toothpicks to keep the fruit in place. This arrangement of fruits and vegetables should last
weeks, even months, depending on your selec-
tion of material and the fact that no one eats
waxed fruits.

HOW TO FINISH DRIFTWOOD

Weathered wood has a natural affinity for
flower decoration, so bring home interesting
pieces of wood and roots from lakes, woods,
and seashore for use as containers, accessories,
and stands. This economy will appeal to you,
as will the sculptured appearance and natural
look of your selections. Few flowers are
needed when you add one of these "rhythm
sticks." When you acquire driftwood in its
native form, you may have to reshape it. This
can be done by sawing off any pieces that
create a busy feeling.

You can buy weathered wood already finished, but if you find your own, it can be used
in its natural state after pouring boiling water
over it to kill any insect life. It can be cloroxed
to change its color. It can be beautifully fin-

ished and waxed to go with your finest furniture. Paint it white, and you will have a centerpiece that can be used as a decoration for your gayest table.

Wash the wood carefully, and allow it to dry thoroughly. Apply a wash made by mixing white or gray casein to a thin solution. Wipe off the excess for the desired effect. For a darker finish, apply stain instead of casein wash. For a highly glossy finish, use varnish and wax. Many pieces sold commercially are buffed by machine.

NATURAL AND STAINED FINISHES FOR DRIFTWOOD

For a natural finish on driftwood, sand the wood until smooth. Brush on two coats of shellac. Rub with steel wool, and then wax or polish with crude oil and rottenstone.

For a stained finish, clean the wood, and sand it until smooth. Apply the stain (can be linseed oil), repeating until the color suits you. (Purchase the desired stain at the paint store, or work on the back of a board with umbers, ochers, Payne's gray, and other oil pigments to perfect the stain desired.) If you want a glossy finish, use white shellac, steel wool, then the stain, and wax.

HOW TO GLAZE STAINED WOOD

To glaze stained wood, sand the cleaned wood, and apply a coat of glaze. Glazes are made of three parts flatting oil and one part turpentine and linseed oil. Oil paints can be added to achieve the desired color. Brush on with a feather-tip brush or a piece of cheesecloth, and allow enough color to remain for the effect you want. In selecting your glazing color, use a neutral, such as gray, with a touch of the color pigment dominant in your composition, such as gray with yellow or gray with red.

Textured finishes may be developed by running steel combs over wood. They come in various sizes to give variety to the graining.

ANTIQUE AND ORIENTAL LACQUER FINISHES

An antique finish similar to metal can be developed by painting the wood with two coats of Venetian red oil pigment and one coat of bronzing gold. Rub with steel wool, and apply a coat of white shellac. Let it dry, and apply a wash of neutral casein. Wipe it, and spatter it lightly with bronzing powder. If silver paint bronzing is used, substitute orange shellac for white shellac.

To give an oriental lacquer finish, smooth the cleaned wood surface with glass paper, which is finer than sandpaper, until it is free from dirt and grease. Prime with one coat of lacquer. When the primer coat is thoroughly dry, apply an undercoating made of fourteen ounces of gilder's whiting and an envelope of ordinary gelatin boiled with one pint of water into a soapy liquid. Allow this to dry, then smooth the surface again with glass paper. Apply the lacquer with broad swift strokes, brushing off runs. Allow it to dry, and repeat the operation five times, allowing one to five hours between each coat, and increasing the time allowance between each coat. When the lacquer dries, rub down with glass paper.

PICKLED WOOD

For pickled wood, carefully sand the cleaned wood, scratching it with diagonal strokes, being careful not to cross them. Apply a series of washes of casein mixed with water into a thin solution. These washes may be white or colored according to the desired finished effect. Wipe or sand the wood for the finished effect. The casein washes may be applied over dried wood stain and then sanded to allow the stain to show through, using the following procedure. First sand, then stain. Apply a coat of white shellac, steel wool, and apply the casein wash. Then sand and wax if a glossy surface is desired. Most bases are better in a dull finish, so they do not draw attention from the arrangement itself.

STANDS GIVE A FINISHED LOOK

In developing a design with driftwood, allow the points of the driftwood to define the outline of your work. Mount the piece of driftwood on a base in an upright, prone, or triangular position. If you elevate your piece by using a small block of wood as a prop, this will emphasize its beauty of form.

An expert look is often given to a simple flower or fruit arrangement by the addition of a stand or base that fits the container in scale, color, and pattern. Stands add height, stability, contrast, and interest to your arrangement and also protect the furniture. If your arrangement is too low, use steps of painted wooden rounds or squares. Footed stands and scrolls are graceful and in keeping with certain styles. Round stands with vertical containers and square stands with round or oval ones give contrast. Such unpretentious objects as old bricks, when suitably used, are possibilities.

Cross sections of tree trunks and roots can be sanded, waxed, and polished. Interesting stands can also be made of weathered.wood and bark. Stone slabs and slate, such as the marble slab that sets off the formal glass container of the arrangement in Plate 41, will improve balance and are appropriate with fine furnishings. Thin lacquered stands with geometric patterns are smart in modern arrangements. Gaily painted tiles and trivets will give a finished look to a Pennsylvania Dutch dish.

DESIGNING PRESSED FLOWER PLAQUES

Bamboo plaques and scrolls in grayed yellow or brown are useful with boat-shaped containers, water-viewing arrangements, and arrangements of fruits and vegetables.

A simple way to press flowers is to place them between the leaves of a heavy book. Cut them in the heat of the day when they have least moisture. First press them between sheets of paper towels. Then lay sheets with pressed leaves between the pages of a book. Weight it down with other books. In two weeks they should be completely pressed and ready for use in plaques. You may combine them with dry plant materials to widen the scope of arrangements. Your design should be consistent with your period of decoration. A quaint bouquet of roses, pansies, Queen Anne's lace, and lupine glued or cemented on maroon velvet or sateen would be Victorian in mood. For a French touch, make gay butterflies of pressed iris petals on a pink fabric. Hang the pictures on velvet ribbons, looped and tied in bows, and use the plaques in groups of two combined with framed pictures to complete a unit.

For modern pictures use seaweed, shells, celosia, bark, driftwood, seed pods, or tritonia. Combine these in bold design, and use grass cloth, burlap, or heavy construction paper for a background.

Sketch your proposed design so you know what plants to gather. Select the picture frame you will use, and cut cardboard or plywood to fit. The frame should be in keeping with your décor and should be simple so as not to detract from the finished picture. Cover the cardboard or wood with the fabric or paper you selected for the background. Stretch it tautly over the selected cardboard or wood, and securely tape or tack it to the back. Lightly sketch in your proposed design. You can transfer completed designs from books. If you wish to include a representation of a vase, either paint or paste additional material to simulate it. Broken bits of eggshell may be cemented to this simulated vase and lacquered to give it the appearance of porcelain.

Starting at the top and working down, carefully secure each piece of material to the cloth or paper, following the sketched pattern and using household cement or glue and tweezers. Overlap the plant material to give body to the completed design. Place some material in profile and some fullface. Expose the pistil of certain flowers, and be sure to graduate the size of the plant materials used. When your plaque is dry, place the glass over it, and attach it to the frame.

Marine materials and scenes lend themselves well to this treatment. Paint in a blue sky, and glue on bits of cotton for clouds. Create a sand beach by painting the foreground with shellac or glue, and sprinkle it with sand. Add shells, sea fans, and bits of coral.

For the children's room, a sugarplum tree panel can be made of dried branches, using pips of roses painted pastel colors and hung on the branches. Autumn leaves dried and rubbed with cream furniture wax will give depth to your tree. Add small birds made of glowing iris petals, their beady eyes of dried berries.

You can make a plaque to place under a glass-topped table. Sentimental flowers from weddings or special mementos can be incorporated into nostalgic decorations. Trays and paperweights can be made in the same way. Patience is an ingredient of success with pressed flowers. Always remember that poor workmanship is magnified under glass.

PLAQUES USING DRIED MATERIALS AND SEED DESIGNS

Dried flowers, fruits, seed pods, and branches can be mounted on wooden panels with the same method as for pressed flowers. The finished panel is not covered with glass, but is given a protective coating of clear shellac. A plywood background can be antiqued by rubbing it with turpentine and linseed oil in equal parts. Dried pomegranates, nuts, and avocado seeds provide interesting forms. Citrous fruits dry beautifully when spiked with cloves. The cloves must cover the fruit completely. Plate 81 shows a modern plaque with a design of sea shells and driftwood. It is easy to see how well such a decoration would fit into a hobby room or modern ranch dining room.

Panel designs can be worked out using only seed. Draw your pattern on the plywood background. Paint with household cement or glue the areas to be seeded. Sprinkle the seeds over the painted areas, creating your pattern by color and form variations. When it is thoroughly dry, coat it with white shellac. Try making a panel of birds in flight for modern décor, using sesame seeds for the background and rice, barley, birdseed, corn, peas, and radish seeds for the rest of the design. Sort the seeds in small cups according to color and kind. Use them as you would colors on an artist's palette. Additional seeds are melon, wistaria, and seeds of flowers.

HOBBY COLLAGES FOR THE FAMILY ROOM

Collages, or paintings that include materials other than paint, were developed by the French abstract painters. You can develop amusing pictures in the same manner, using bright bits of fabrics, paper, miniature figurines, or whatever you wish, in addition to plant materials. They can be framed in glass or shellacked. It is fun to decorate a playroom wall with collages, depicting the hobbies and pleasures of each member of the family. Mounted butterflies, sea shell collections, or shellacked panels of colorful postage stamps combined with dry grasses and leaves create conversational interests.

For an Early American interior, you may wish to try a fireside scene. Select a nicely grained piece of plywood the desired size for the completed picture. Divide it into floor and wall area by pasting a baseboard of colored paper or wood at the desired level. Braid a little rug of yarn or scraps, and glue it in the center of the floor. Glue slivers of wood to simulate a mantel and hearth. (Elmers glue is a good all-purpose glue.) Paint or paste bits of paper for hearth bricks between the slivers of wood. Glue in a fireside grouping small pieces of doll furniture painted to echo the period. Paste a cut-out clock or picture over the mantel. A fuzzy cotton pussycat can be added to the scene. A paper book in a chair and perhaps a pair of wire spectacles on a table will give a lived-in look to your collage. When you have allowed all materials to dry thoroughly, cover them with a clear lacquer. Frame the plywood in black tape, or use a wooden frame with a cardboard back. You can have fun by adding other small objects of paper, cloth, plastic, or other material, such as a kettle by the fire. You can repaint them or recover them. Outdoor scenes of apple picking, sugaring off, or supper at grandma's would provide groupings for a wall.

A DELIGHTFULLY FRAGRANT POTPOURRI

Although essentially potpourri is functional, serving to perfume a room delightfully, charming apothecary jars filled with pastel mixtures of flower petals are decorative, too.

Gather newly opened blossoms on a dry sunny day, discarding the stems and leaves and using only the petals. Herbs should be gathered at their aromatic best, which is just before flowering. Use only the leaves. In the covers of cardboard boxes, spread all your material thinly, and leave it in a warm dry room for two or three days, stirring the material once a day.

When drying is completed, place the petals or foliage in layers in storage jars. Sprinkle a light layer of salt between each layer of petals, and add a few drops of oil of rose. When you have enough dried material, you are ready for the blending. Add the spices, and stir well with a wooden spoon. Fill your potpourri jars with the mixture, and cover tightly. Keep the jars closed except when you wish to perfume the room.

VI

Decorations with pot plants

BRIGHTENING THE DAYS OF WINTER ARE MANY familiar house plants. Begonias, geraniums, and other flowers brought color to the December scene as they grew alongside fern and ivy in the bay windows of grandmother's home. Today these blooms still accent special places, along the tops of bookcases, growing in wall planters, or brightening mantels and tables.

While their delicacy is appropriate to period homes, plants with bolder forms—bromeliads, dracaenas, bamboo, and dwarf palm —seem better fitted to the modern tempo. Indoor gardens that begin at the door and continue through the hallway to the stairs (Plates 85 and 98) require plants that act important and look handsome the year round. Modern plantings should fit the space they are to occupy and, like sculpture, look well from all angles.

RELATING HOUSE PLANTS TO OBJECTS AROUND THEM

House plants must be related to the objects around them. As with flower arrangements, containers for plants should harmonize in spirit with the rest of the room. A bronze bowl with a pot of aspidistra enhances a home decorated in the Oriental manner. A collection of cacti and succulents in a natural wood container belongs in a southwestern ranch house. A milk glass compote holding trailing ivy seems right with colonial styles. These are happy blendings of container, plant, and decoration.

Colors must harmonize too. The color in the plant material no longer need be left to chance. You can plant material in almost any color, but to insure a match, take fabric and plant samples when you shop. A well-dressed room reflects such painstaking attention to detail. The clay pot can be used in its familiar hue, or it can be painted with enamel house paint (flat paint will chip) to match the rest of the room. Bamboo, grass cloth, or Con-tact can be fitted to the pot or attached at the back. If glazed or decorated pots do not allow for soil aeration and drainage, put a layer of pebbles in the bottom to improve the drainage before you add the soil.

Figures, ornaments, and natural accessories such as driftwood, shells, and stones help sus-

85. *Transition from outdoors to in is accomplished in this planting area which is planted on both sides of an exterior glass wall. Tropical plant material and a small rock garden will stay healthy and decorative the year round with sun, water and some plant food. In the home of Mrs. Henry Kirschenbaum. (Photo by Gottscho-Schleisner)*

86. *An English planter lined with waterproofed metal includes pots of dieffenbachia, aucuba and pothos which require little light. Once a week plants are taken to the kitchen for a thorough watering. In the home of Mrs. Norman Arons. (Photo by Gottscho-Schleisner)*

tain the mood in a room, but nothing is more tiresome than the same little figurine displayed month after month or year after year in the same old way. Rest the Staffordshire figure now and then, and try in its place a pretty ceramic cat, a group of cherubs at Christmas, or a handsome witch for Halloween. Even your hobbies can add personality to window plantings, as does the glass collection in Plate 88.

FUNCTIONAL PLANTING

Whether you choose small plants or large ones, plantings have far more function than in the past. They solve decorating and architectural problems. For instance, trailing plants unite two separate areas, such as a mantel and the furniture grouped below it, or as in Plate 96 the two parts of a modern window wall. And not only can plants unite areas, but they can separate them or function as dividers in open-plan homes (Plates 95, 97, and 105).

Since plants need light, they cannot always be grown where most needed. In a dark hall, colorful blooms may be moved in from porch or window for special occasions. Or to summerize a fireplace, foliage plants can be arranged around hearth ornaments before guests arrive, as in Plate 89, and be moved back into sunlight the following morning.

BUILT-IN PLANTERS

Formerly, built-in planters were used chiefly outdoors, but as fieldstone, slate, and brick came inside, planters followed. Now, wooden tubs, rough terra cotta, massive cast concrete, and glazed tile boxes are used for interiors,

whatever the outside. All planters must be lined with metal but not copper unless painted with asphaltum paint. For good drainage about two inches of pebbles should go at the bottom of the planter. They must be near a window or have provision for artificial light (Plate 90). Otherwise, the pots should be moved into the light for several hours a day.

Such plants as poinsettias need protection against temperature drops if growing near windows; others, such as aspidistras, against severe cold. Freezing weather outside often results in marked temperature drops near a window inside. A milium-lined drapery, or aluminum foil, or a newspaper covering between plant and window at night will insulate against extreme cold.

If a radiator must serve as the base for your window garden, put a sheet of asbestos or a thick layer of rock wool on the radiator cover to insulate against the heat. Top with a shallow metal tray lined with sand or pebbles, and water the garden daily. Keep about one-quarter inch of water on the pebbles all the time. A humidifier, bought at a hardware store, can be hung behind the radiator.

If built-on or built-in planters are not available, you can find attractive stands, tier tables, teacarts, brackets, hanging baskets, fanciful bird cages, lavaboes, and similar objects to fit almost any type of decoration.

PLANTS FOR EARLY AMERICAN AND PROVINCIAL ROOMS

The African violet, though not used until well into the present century, seems perfectly at home in color and form with Early American rooms..We are not concerned here with plantings for historical accuracy, but with combi-

87. *Brightening a little girl's room (it would be appropriate in an informal dining room too) this antique dry sink is gaily planted with geraniums, philodendron and ivy. The red checked wallpaper repeats the color of the geraniums and contrasts with the blue Meissen plates. In the home of Mrs. Millard Rothenberg. (Photo by Gottscho-Schleisner)*

88. *At the window of an Early American home geraniums and a glass collection are a cheerful sight in winter. In the home of Mrs. William Herrmann. (Photo by Gottscho-Schleisner)*

nations that are right in today's period and modern homes.

In an Early American den, an earthenware bean pot filled with pot marigold is appropriate against pine paneling, as are sprigs of grape ivy swinging from a hobnailed glass lamp. A modern translation of the rural feeling can be a black wrought-iron pin-up planter lamp with a rooster base, the lamp providing the light necessary for the growth of the trailing plant material. Such articles as a copper kettle on a trivet, spice boxes, and spoon racks are all possible planters for Provincial rooms. An Early American sink has been transformed into an indoor flower center (Plate 87), and even recessed cobbler benches and an old spinning wheel (Plate 94) can take up new functions. Azaleas, primroses, wax begonias, or caladium leaves will look well in a tall Victorian shaving mug. In the same period, a bird cage planted with the spider plant seems completely at home. Gardens under glass described later in this chapter are suitable.

PLANTS FOR LOUIS XVI OR REGENCY SETTINGS

For a French Louis XVI or Regency setting, massed ferns and wax begonias, which do well in a subdued light, or a dwarf espalier fruit tree, which needs sun, are suitable. Provin-

cial rooms with Oriental overtones are attractively planted with pots of cyclamen in fluted pewter.

You can grow a lemon, grapefruit, or orange tree. Plant the seed within an hour after it is taken from the fruit in a four- or five-inch pot holding ordinary potting soil. It takes three to five weeks to sprout, but may take years to bloom. In the meantime, enjoy the satiny foliage. When roots crowd the pot, transplant to larger pot or small wooden tub. When the plant is about two feet high, which may take several years, it may be espaliered. Train it on a wire or wood frame in the desired shape. This frame is put in the pot behind the plant. As the plant grows, tie it to the frame with wire, thread, string, or raffia. Be careful not to bruise the plant.

Potted fruit trees grown at home or bought from the florist, or any climbing plant such as ivy, may be trained against wire or wood supports into these different shapes.

89. *Philodendron and begonia plants placed in an umbrella stand behind the fire chenets summerize an elegant French fireplace. (Photo by Gottscho-Schleisner)*

Small glass bowls, suspended from slender chains and filled with forced lily of the valley pips can be used in a room with French décor. Wrought-iron and reed baskets help make these fixtures suitable for use in family recreation rooms as well as outdoors on terrace settings.

In elegant rooms in gray and white with golden accents, perhaps, an exotic planting of fancy-leaved green, gray, and white caladium leaves combined with silvery gray and rex be-

gonias is lovely. Begonia Angel Wing planted in a chased brass Persian water bucket or Chinese evergreen and Ficus quercifolia in a Chinese bowl on a teakwood stand fit in with the Eastern mood. Camellias echo the feeling of old lotus paintings in Chinese prints and are dramatic placed on large black lacquer tables.

RELIEVING STARKNESS OF MODERN DÉCOR

To relieve the starkness of modern furniture, trailing plants are useful. In a solar house, plants grow luxuriously and hardily. Dramatic forms of palm and croton are particularly attractive when silhouetted against a window. Here, cacti and succulents are also at home, since they are not only decorative in form but easy to take care of. Succulents and other desert plants such as sedum, sempervivium, and euphorbia are frequently grouped to form interesting desert scenes. These plants need little water; they are filled with juicy tissue that is moisture-storing. Generally, cacti and succulents are more effective in groupings rather than as single-specimen potted plants along a window sill. Some cacti produce bright flowers. The orchid cactus, for example, has many varieties that bear large blossoms in red, white, pink, orange, and crimson.

For a contemporary breakfast room decorated with pink wrought iron, geranium Mrs. Nelson Eddy (pink), with variegated ivy, geranium (green and white), and velvet plant (green) are lovely. Or feature a collection of pink and purple African violets (see list later in this chapter). For pink wrought iron, you can also use double-flowered begonia Snow White with jasmine gracillimum and rex begonia Solid Silver.

90. *Fluorescent lighting built into a cove in this modern living room assures good growth for the plants which are an essential part of the decoration. (Courtesy Armstrong Linoleum Co.)*

A modern recreation room in the basement or a converted front porch can have imaginative plants. A wooden teacart painted in vivid colors and covered with a striped awning can hold African violets, geraniums, petunias, begonias, and trailing plants such as pothos, creeping fig, or syngonium. Fluorescent lights concealed under the awning will insure plant vitality. In Plate 91, an Italian Provincial teacart forms a gay setting that can be moved around the house as needed for decoration or sun. Wheels fixed to a gaily painted old bachelor chest makes a practical cart, or in an outdoor setting an old wheelbarrel is useful.

In modern homes, cleaned tree stumps, branches, and driftwood are exciting, as described in Chapter V. They are charming planted with orchids, fern, and palm. When planting with Cymbidium orchids, hollow out pockets in the driftwood to fit the size of your plant. Prepare a mixture of top soil and sand in equal parts. Add to this a little peat moss and ground wood chips. Plant the orchids in the pockets of the driftwood using the prepared mixture as a growing agent. Remember the roots are moisture-storing, so water with moderation. The driftwood can be placed in a planter or on a tray to catch drainage. These same gardens can be incorporated into water gardens in a playroom.

RELATING PLANT COLOR AND TEXTURE TO ROOM FABRICS

In a French Provincial family den furnished in earth browns and tans, and if the room fabric is nubby, consider such colorful rough-textured plants as begonia Angel Wing combined with philodendron wenlandi and philodendron cordatum or pelargonium Salmon Splendor, used with grape ivy or wandering Jew. Coleus and caladium in a less-textured room will add needed interest. Try not to mix red-violets with orange unless you have Mexican décor.

In a brown and tan room, in which smoother textures are needed, try an all-green planting with an accent of yellow, as in dieffenbachia Rudolph Roehrs, or green-gold nephthytis with oxalis and wax plant.

In rooms with blues and violets predominating, consider African violets Velvet Beauty and Purple Prince. Orchid plants during their blooming period are spectacular for these rooms. An all-green planting with an accent

91. *A contemporary teacart on a slate terrace holds potted plants on the top shelf and fruits and flowers below. The lavabo is filled with pots of Pittsburgh ivy and a branch of yew. In the home of Mrs. Henry Kirschenbaum. (Photo by Gottscho-Schleisner)*

92.   *An Italian gold compote with waterproof liner, planted with living greens (aspidistra, Philodendron oxycardium and pothos), is accented by one red anthurium. Arranged by Mrs. Ward Wright. (Photo by Panda)*

of rex begonia Patsy or Heteor would be lovely. Blue plumbago framing a planter of spring bulbs, such as yellow daffodils, pink, blue, and purple tulips and hyacinths, give a glorious spring feeling to a color scheme of blue or violet. (Cheap bulbs are poor economy. It is wise to pay more and get better bulbs.)

Don't overlook the textural value of house plants. Fine fabrics and furnishings invite delicate plant material. Country cousins reflect house plant charm with coarser materials. Texture may be added to a room with plain surfaces by using house plants rex begonia, cacti, or philodendron pandreamum.

SELECTING HOUSE PLANTS BY COLOR

PLANT	SPECIES OR VARIETY	COLOR
African violet	Purity	white
African violet	Snow Prince	white
Apostle plant	Madonna	white
Azalea	Niobe	white
Begonia	Dainty Maid	white
Begonia	Snowbank	white
Begonia	Snow White	white
Begonia, rex	Solid Silver	white
Begonia, tuberous	Santa Marie	white
Geranium	Snowball	white
Pelargoniums	Gay Nineties	white
Petunia	Snowstorm	white
Begonia	Limminghei	coral
African violet	Amazon pink	pink
Begonia	Angel Wing	salmon-pink
Begonia	Cinderella	pink
Begonia	Ernest K.	pink-rose
Begonia, hanging	Lloydi	pink
Begonia, tuberous	Santa Margarita	pink
Geranium	American Beauty	rose
Geranium	Pink Giant	pink
Geranium, ivy leaf	Charles Turner	pink
Geranium, trailing	Beach Blow	pink
Impatiens		pink
Petunia	Cheerful	pink
Begonia	Red Pearl	red
Begonia, tuberous	Red Triumph	red
Christmas cactus		rose-red
Geranium	Berkeley Brilliant	deep red
Geranium	Better Times	crimson red
Kalanchoe	Brilliant Star	red
Aeschynanthus pulcher		waxy green
Aralia		green
Acuba		green and yellow
Caladium	Machahyba	green and violet
Caladium	Mixed varieties	green with rainbow colors
Dieffenbachia		green and yellow-green
Dracaena		green with yellow or red stripes
Evergreen, Chinese		green
Ivy		green
Ivy	Gold Dust	green, white, and yellow
Kalanchoe	Yellow Darling	green with yellow flowers
Maple, flowering		green or bronze
African violet	Blue Fairy Tale	blue
African violet	Blue Heiress	blue
African violet	Sailor Girl	blue
Morning-glory	Heavenly Blue	blue
Petunia	Blue Bird	violet-blue
Plumbago capensis		blue

93.   A basement is converted into this lovely sunken garden room. Lush potted plants and colorful annuals grown indoors help create an out-of-doors atmosphere and bring the freshness of nature into a room devoted to family living. Start the annuals in December or January. Fill a five-inch pot with a mixture of equal amounts of sand, humus and garden soil. Plant five or six seeds in a 5-inch pot. When each seedling has two sets of leaves, thin out to 2 or 3 in a pot. Feed once a week with a good fertilizer, Water and about five hours of sun. The following are good to grow from seed:
VINES: *Blackeyed Susan (thunbergia alata), Morning glory, Heavenly Blue, Nasturtiums, (climbing).* POTTED ANNUALS: *Calendula, flowering maple (Abutilon), French marigolds. (Courtesy Armstrong Linoleum Co.)*

PLANT	SPECIES OR VARIETY	COLOR
African violet	Ruffled Queen	burgundy-violet
African violet	Wine Velvet	burgundy-violet
African violet	Lavender Beauty	violet
African violet	Orchid Wonder	violet
African violet	Violet Beauty	violet
Begonia, rex	Metallic	silvery violet
Gloxinias	Emperor Wilhelm	violet
Lantana, trailing		rose lilac
Pelargonium	Troubadour Violet	violet
Begonia, tuberous	Sunset Copper	copper-orange
Cactus	Flamingo	copper-orange
Clivia		salmon orange
Geranium	Honeymoon	salmon orange
Petunia	Tango	scarlet orange
Begonia	Mazae	bronze with white flowers
Begonia	Scharffianna	bronze
Episcia fulgida		bronze
Strelitzia	Reginae	green leaves, blue and orange flowers

94. *A charming spinning wheel is an imaginative planter, well related to the other ornaments in this Early American home. Potted philodendron is twined around the wheel. In the home of Mrs. William Herrmann. (Photo by Gottscho-Schleisner)*

CHOOSING PLANTS FOR SCALE AND FORM

House plants may also be chosen for their scale and form. Screw pine, for example, is a moderately scaled plant for pot culture, although in its native habitat, the islands of the Pacific, it grows into a tall tree. It is very symmetrical and is seen to its best advantage when viewed in the round, so use it in an open space rather than against a wall.

Dieffenbachia, with its very large leaf, adds tropic lushness to a room. Since each leaf has a large distinct form, the plant should not be crowded and is attractive viewed across a room.

Sometimes a low-growing plant that will bear close inspection is wanted, as for a coffee table. For this, Sylvanian Beauty ivy offers smooth, even green leaves, symmetrically arranged.

For vivacity and showiness, try fancy-leafed caladiums, which offer many color patterns such as leaves with pink dots of all sizes or pink leaves with green edges. Amaryllis also is exceedingly showy, giving big bold flowers with little care.

The following plants are easy to grow. They need light but no sun.

Begonias (flowering plant)
Cacti and other succulents
Chinese evergeen (foliage plant)
Dieffenbachia (foliage)
Geraniums (flowering plant)
Helxine soleiroli (baby tears) (foliage)
Inch plant
Ivy vine (English, and grape varieties)
Philodendron (vine, many varieties)
Pickaback plant (foliage plant)
Wandering Jew (vine)

HERB GARDENS AND OTHER PLANTINGS FOR THE KITCHEN

In a sunny kitchen, though not necessarily in a window with all-day sunshine, a quaint herb garden can be grown. It is important, however, that herbs be raised in an area free of drafts and gas fumes. On stepped-up shelves in the window, try anise, coriander, dill, mallow, and chervil. Another interesting grouping is thyme, burnet, lavender, and rosemary. In a less sunny spot, place pots of hyssop, mints, and woodruff. An all-gray effect may be obtained by growing santolina, lavender, horehound, sage, and artemisia. Annual herbs are ambrosia, sweet basil, sweet fennel, sweet marjoram, sweet mugwort, anise, borage, dill, German camomile, false saffron, and sweet summer savory. Herbs may be grown from seeds, or seedlings can be bought at nurseries.

Under a shelf or in a corner cabinet with fluorescent lighting, you can grow African violets, aralia elegantissima, and ferns such as pteris, fittonia, bird's-nest, and holly fern.

In a partial sun area, an attractive planting can be made of arrow plant, bowstring hemp (sansevieria), dracaena, fittonia, and philodendron. Try growing these in a small wall planter incorporating a picture on the wall, a lamp on the table, or other accessories, into the balance of the planter. Sunlight may be replaced by fluorescent light from above.

Try hanging an empty picture frame with a shelf on its edge. Recess into the frame begonias and vining grape ivy. Place a picture light above it for the supplementary lighting required for proper plant growth.

The kitchen of tomorrow with heatless cooking will broaden the scope for plants in this room. In modern kitchens, the importance of the window over the sink, increased counter space, and a less clinical approach make this room a natural place for plants. The elegant new colors of cabinets, stoves, and refrigerators—shrimp pink, light clear yellow, Williamsburg blue, and others—invite skill in harmonizing appliances and plants.

An intriguing hobby in the kitchen is to grow only the scented geraniums, such as nutmeg, cinnamon, lavender, lemon peppermint, and anise. Plate 99 is an example of an Early American kitchen with potted herbs and a large burl bowl used as a planter. You can use herbal leaves in food preparation or to scent your bath. They are hardy plants and will grow even in poor soil, but they like dry feet. Natural gas is generally believed not to be harmful to plants, but escaping manufactured gas is lethal to plants. Geraniums and sansevieria seem to be able to withstand kitchen conditions.

PLANTS FOR BATHROOM AND NURSERY

House plants are finding their way into rooms new to them. For example, in modern bathrooms the counter washbowl has taken the place of the rimless basin where there was no room for even a toothbrush. Now, potted plants and flower arrangements seem to belong on the mosaic tile, structural glass, and plastic surfaces. Here, where heat and moisture are high, orchids do well as house plants. Glass shelves with clear glass bottles filled with water in which ivy, wandering Jew, or dracaena is growing are suitable for a bathroom. A tiled planter used as a room divider can be effectively planted with tropical materials. Fluorescent light, left burning for supplementary light, insures good growth. Also for a bathroom, try placing a redwood burl, bark side up, in a low flat dish containing water. (Your florist can order one for you.) They only last a year but are very interesting to watch grow.

The child's bedroom or nursery, now receiving attention for its value in developing a love of learning and beauty in the growing child, offers a worth-while location for growing plants and terrariums. House plants allow a child to study the plant cycle on a daily basis. Children find pleasure in watching a sweet potato sprout and vine in a window. Cut off the end of a sprouting potato, and place the potato in a glass so that the cut end is immersed in water. Keep cool and dark for a week, then transfer it to a light place, where your child can watch the roots grow in the water. A spoonful of dried lentil beans or an avocado seed can also be grown. Start in water then transfer to a pot of soil when they sprout.

WATER GARDENS, LAVABOES, TERRACE PLANTERS

The combination of running water with growing plants, so popular in Japanese residential architecture, has a special fascination. On ter-

PLANTS AS ROOM DIVIDERS

95. (Opposite above) Open planning in modern home design has increased the need for space dividers. Here small-leaved ivy trailing from built-in planters at the ceiling visually separates barbecue-fireplace from terrace dining area. Planters at windows assure sunlight but pots must be taken down at least once a week and watered thoroughly. (Courtesy Armstrong Linoleum Co.)

96. (Opposite below) A tall planting of monstera deliciosa in a corner draws attention to the steps leading from living room to dining room. At the base, small potted philodendrons which can withstand poor light hide the large pot. (Courtesy Armstrong Linoleum Co.)

97. Here a planting of philodendron oxycardium, requiring little light, softens the severe contours of the room divider which contains a metal liner for pots. In the home of Mrs. Ben Burnette. (Photo by Jack Thurman)

races, sun porches, or in large entrance halls, small corner pools are architecturally exciting. The iridescence of fish scales and the color and form of water plants and surrounding potted plants add beauty to a serene scene. Water pools may be built into rough-cut stone walls in the entrance to a modern home and be lighted to dramatize surrounding plantings of tropical foliage.

In period homes of French and Italian influence, wall fountains and lavaboes are delightful. A lavabo can be filled with perfumed water or with fish, or planted with trailing plants of philodendron, ivy, wandering Jew, or lantana. Pots of geraniums, coleus, or herbs can be used for accent.

In Plate 2, a contemporary entrance hall is given dramatic impact and seems to make a transition from outdoors to indoors with a cleverly planted water garden using a Japanese motif.

Plant boxes and terrace gardens for Early American, French Provincial, and Dutch Colonial homes suggest informal plant material such as spring bulbs, pink and red geraniums, and strawberry begonias.

For a ranch home, dramatic effects may be obtained by using driftwood as a container or support for vines. Hollow out a pocket in the wood, have it lined with metal, and plant African violets, ivy, philodendron, or fuchsias in the pockets. Or place the driftwood upright in a pot, and train the plants over it. The driftwood gives a sculptured quality to the plant.

COMBINING ARTIFICIAL LIGHT WITH SUNLIGHT

Your plants need either sun or artificial light —incandescent bulbs, fluorescent ones, or a combination. Two 40-watt tubes placed twelve inches above your plants will light a bench one foot wide and three feet long. Do not have the lights on more than twelve to eighteen hours a day.

The few favorites listed below will give you an idea of the light needed for various plants. The hours are based on approximately 70-degree day temperature and 60-degree night temperature. Regulate the artificial light by the amount of sunlight that the plant receives. To determine the amount of supplementary artificial light you may need, study the progress of your plant material as it grows.

These plants do well with ten hours of light a day: aspidistra, dracaena, dieffenbachia, philodendron, and sansevieria.

These plants do well with approximately twelve hours of light a day: bromeliads, fern, holly, maranta (prayer plant), and peperomia.

These plants do well with approximately fifteen hours of light a day: cacti, croton, fuchsia, and pelargonium (geranium).

(See also page 197.)

BASEMENT NURSERY FOR PLANTS

As you become more interested in plants, you may wish to develop a nursery in the basement to nurture and propagate replacements for planters.

The plants should be placed near enough to the furnace to maintain the needed temperatures during the winter. The garden consists of adjustable trays on a movable aluminum rack. (Many nurserymen sell these.) The trays are filled with pebbles, and an inch of water is kept on them. A clock turns lights on and off, allowing plants on separate trays their needed hours of light. Since flowers need both blue and red rays, use two 40-watt daylight fluorescent tubes and two 25-watt incandescent bulbs. It is not necessary, however, to so regulate the rays. It merely perfects the growing conditions.

The advantages of this basement culture are numerous, considering its artificiality. The authors have found, for example, that base-ment moisture is an asset to plant growth. Pest control is simpler than it is outdoors. Such exotic plants (for our northern climate) as dwarf orange trees and even melons do well under fluorescent light. We rotate the house plants, allowing so many weeks upstairs in their planters and so many weeks in the

98.   *A passageway in a contemporary home features trailing begonia (Cissus discolor) which frames the figurine and is related texturally to the mother-of-pearl walls. (Photo by Gottscho-Schleisner)*

99.   *Potted herbs belong in this Early American scene with a mold, frying pan, measures, and a bird cage to stress the homely theme. The herbs are anise, coriander, dill, chervil, mint, parsley and woodruff. Arranged by Mrs. William L. Kleitz. (Photo by Hugelmeyer)*

100.   *An improvised kitchen greenhouse, above right, reminds a busy housewife to tend her plants! Pots in full bloom can be moved to other places in the home where decoration is needed. (Courtesy Armstrong Linoleum Co.)*

101. *(Lower right)   Ivy climbs along the window of a modern kitchen from a pot hung in the upper left, and pothos trails from a shelf above the cookbooks and desk. At the far wall, a few simple flowers are casually arranged in a bowl. (Courtesy Armstrong Linoleum Co.)*

basement nursery. Here they receive extra "shots of sunshine" according to the needs of their variety. African violets are highly successful in basement culture. They can reach their maximum bloom cycle under fluorescent light. Finally, plants grown under artificial light appear well rounded in shape. (Plants grown in window light achieve this form only by daily turning of the pots.)

GARDENS UNDER GLASS

Terrariums, gardens in glass, usually suggest Victorian décor, since the bell jar was a favor-

102. *Terrariums make interesting decorations for a family den or a child's room. All the mosses, tiny trees, and lichens in this one were lifted from wooded mountains in New York State, and one tiny lily imbedded in the moss bloomed for a full week after! Instructions for making a terrarium are on this page. Arranged by Mrs. William Y. Boyd. (Photo by Hugelmeyer)*

ite Victorian accessory, used as a dust protector for faded souvenir bouquets, figurines, and other treasures. Since French and English styles do mix well with Victorian, these glass domes filled with vivid plants are highly decorative accessories for these periods. The type of glass used (it can vary from bottle to cake dish, from goldfish bowl to goblet) suggests the period. A brass coachman's lantern for example, bracketed to the wall, can be an unusual terrarium for a Federal room. Similarly, for a lavish formal note, great glass sconces can be planted as terrariums. In a modern room, a bottle terrarium can give a touch of *trompe-l'oeil* (fool the eye) magic to the scene. Chunky contemporary glassware is most effective used as containers. This is one way, too, to use a beautiful glass pitcher that cracked.

Small evergreen materials are best for a terrarium or dish garden, as shown in Plate 102, where a whole woodsy world in miniature has been created. The materials may be obtained from the roadside, backyard, or greenhouse. Making a terrarium is not difficult. First, put moss topside down in the bottom of the container, extending it up the sides to cover the bottom completely. Cover this with leaf mold, and place the plants according to the desired design. Miniature Japanese gardens are charming, and the addition of figurines, small rocks, and bits of wood are interesting. In choosing materials, select those that are moisture-loving. African violets, helxine soleiroli, caladiums, begonias, crotons, miniature ivy, fittonia, and moss achieve green glossy foliage and healthy blooms.

Cover the planted container with a piece of glass or clear plastic. The main problem in a terrarium is moisture regulation. This is accomplished by simply lifting the glass top from time to time. If too much moisture is

103. *Trailing English Ivy (attached with Vintacks) and colorful geraniums, soften a fence which secures privacy for a small terrace. Doorway planting by the Litchfield Garden Club. (Photo by Hugelmeyer)*

Dish gardens require little care and can be fun for children. A cowboy garden of cacti and sand growing in a pie tin is an engrossing playroom decoration. A small figure of a bucking horse on a mound of sand carries out the story.

For a cool spot, such as a shady porch, you can also create a woodland garden composed of the smallest plants found in the woods in your area. These might include evergreen seedlings, violets, hepatica, mosses, and small fern. Be sure, however, that none of the plants used are among those protected by the conservation department of your state.

INSURING GOOD LOOKS FOR HOUSE PLANTS

A neglected house plant is poor decoration. The following suggestions will help you attain healthy plants.

1. Provide sunlight according to variety. Keep the plants in a draft-free area with fresh air circulation.

2. Water your plants regularly. A general rule is a good soaking once a week.

3. Give supplementary feeding of commercial plant food following the directions on the package.

4. Proper light, water, and feeding according to the needs of your plants are the best methods of preventing plant pests and diseases. Wash your plants with water and mild soap. At the first sign of aphids, spider mites, thrips, or white flies, spray with D-X Aero-Spray. Mealybugs are small white sucking insects. They attack many house plants. At the first sight of their fluffy white bodies, wash the plants, and try to pick off the bugs with a

104. *Just inside the terrace shown in Plate 103, potted and cut geraniums, below an Early American sampler, relate the interior setting to the one outdoors. Arranged by Mrs. Ralph P. Manny. (Photo by Hugelmeyer)*

permitted to evaporate, the garden must be carefully watered so it does not dry out. The plants will re-use the condensed moisture in their plant cycle.

105. (Opposite) *A room divider in a modern apartment holds art objects and plants of potted pothos. An arrangement on the table includes seed pods of the Cedrus atlantica, glaucoa with a root for line interest. Arranged by Blanche Scarlett Phelps, in the home of Mr. and Mrs. David Weitz.*

toothpick dipped in alcohol, or use an oil spray under the manufacturer's directions. (Do not use an oil spray on African violets or other house plants with hairy leaves.) Plant pests are divided into two types—sucking and chewing. Use stomach poisons for chewing insects and a contact spray for sucking ones. Overwatering plants may cause rots. With rots and nematodes, which infect the soil, it is best to discard the plant and the soil and start over again.

5. If roots are crowded (coming through the bottom of the pot) re-pot the plant in a larger pot, adding more potting mixture around the plant. Keep the soil one-half inch below the rim of the pot to allow for watering. When plants grow leggy, start new plants from cuttings. (See propagation from cuttings.)

Bonsai, or dwarfed trees, can be conversation pieces for the home. They can be purchased at the Brooklyn Botanic Garden, Brooklyn, New York. Information on their care also can be procured there.

VII

Flowers, key to table beauty

A WELL-PLANNED FLORAL DECORATION IS THE center of interest on any table. It unifies china, silver, and linen, and when properly designed, relates all appointments to the period décor. For the contemporary hostess, the centerpiece is an opportunity to be clever by tying in the menu with the table design. A Chinese supper party with a centerpiece such as illustrated in Plate 106 starts off looking like fun. And a practical reason for taking pains with flowers is that beautiful settings make the simplest meals seem interesting. If a Very Important Person is an unexpected guest, you can give an air of ceremony and welcome even to a casual frozen-food meal by a properly planned centerpiece.

NEW SCENES AND TABLE COMPOSITIONS

The lovely new vistas that picture windows have opened for us, and the urge to follow the winter and summer sun through the house as we dine, have made "dining areas" of many rooms. The formal eighteenth-century mahog-

any dining room will keep its lovely place, but the family den, terrace, or lanai, and buffet set at the fireplace are increasingly a part of the dining picture. Everywhere, mealtimes are made more beautiful with lovely table compositions that relate to the room in which they are used.

Your appointments get a new lift by a change of color or texture. Remember that any color used on your table must be compatible with the general scheme of the room. If you have flowered draperies, make solid-color mats to match the dominant flower. If you are tired of your Spode, change the color scheme of the linen. Test analogous harmony; try a contrasting texture of nubby woven cotton place mats or Lurex cloth to bring out the creamy smoothness of the Spode. Or if your set seems heavy, use only the dinner plates and add glass coupettes and goblets. For change developed through rhythm, repeat a color from your Spode in the cloth, flowers, and candles.

A tablecloth and napkins can be dyed to harmonize with one of the background hues in your china. Such co-ordination of color is well worth the effort it takes. If you are planning a table in which two hues will be used, dye the cloth the less vivid color. Save the brighter hue for floral accent. Follow directions on the dye package for method.

The shape of the table should have some general relationship to the room. A refectory table for the long narrow dining room and an oval or a round table for the square room seem most pleasing. If the chair seats are covered with patterned fabrics, keep the walls or floors simple. For snack meals a nest of tables supplies needed space.

HARMONIZING TABLE APPOINTMENTS AND DECORATION

In shopping for table accessories, consider a simple design in flat silver, particularly if your china is ornate. Supplement your good china with special accessories. Fried chicken in gilded baskets, arroz con pollo in individ-

106. *Simplicity and charm characterize this setting for a party featuring an Oriental menu. The decoration is a single water lily (a dahlia or a few roses would do) placed in a pincup between two pearl shells. Iridescence in the shells is echoed in the figurines and the gray and white plates. Black bowls are lined with white. Grass cloth wallpaper is the table covering. Arranged by Anabel Combs Lasker. (Photo by Gottscho-Schleisner)*

107. *Old and new accessories add flavor to this setting in a provincial room with a lazy Susan pine table. An old pewter basket holds black grapes, mustard-colored yarrow, golden arborvitae, and russet leaves of the saxifrage megasea. Modern gray plates by Russel Wright are set on black service plates. Chartreuse cups and saucers, powder blue napkins, and replicas of Early American pewter beakers and porringers complete an unusual color scheme. Arranged by Esther Wheeler.*

ual gay Mexican casseroles, scalloped fish in shells—these make your parties fun. If you are buying new china, it is modern and lively to vary the pattern for each course. But even one pattern can be made interesting with different cloths, napkins, flowers, containers, and candles. With a color wheel, work out analogous, monochromatic, and complementary harmonies.

To give personality to a floral design and make it suitable in period, form, and scale to your table, add accessories that keep the same mood of formality or informality. Containers should be related in color, texture, and period to the décor of the room. (Chapter II has many suggestions.)

A decoration placed in the center of a table should be low enough to permit vision and conversation across the table. A round bowl, a low horizontal dish, or such deeper dishes as a cake basket, vegetable dish, or soup tureen are suitable. A small footed stand under a low container gives a finished look. A pincup (metal dish large enough to hold water and including a pinholder) is on the market. You can put one on a board with your flowers in it and eliminate a container.

Containers devised from wooden kitchen utensils, small coffee grinders, scales, and small mirrors set in a baking dish are unique and appropriate for barbecues and other informal meals.

108.   *The piquant figurine is an important part of this table decoration. Woven mats of mauve linen pick up the color of the grapes in the Old Vine pattern. Gray glasses repeat the gray of the figurine. An arrangement of pandanus foliage (cut from a house plant), lavender chrysanthemums, gray-green echeveria, and purple begonia leaves, complete a contemporary table. Arranged by Anabel Combs Lasker. (Photo by Boutrelle-Sevecke)*

Silver containers, fine linen, and fine crystal belong together. When using a glass or crystal bowl, lay a few leaves sideways around the pinholder to mask it. Shells, teapots, gravy boats, baskets, and compotes all make lovely containers.

Tall containers are useful when the table is pushed back against a wall and the decoration placed in the rear center. When the prevailing mood is elegance, make your table arrangement higher than eye level when the guests are seated, and sufficiently airy so that vision and conversation are not discouraged.

MAKING OR DECORATING CANDLES

Your candles should be related in size, color, and texture to the rest of your table. Very interesting results can be obtained by pouring hot wax into a section of drainpipe for molds. If you do not wish to make the entire candle, use a smooth surfaced candle, and add melted wax. Melt a little at a time and as it cools to a setting point, quickly apply it to the side of

109. *A trip to the greengrocer will produce most of the material for this centerpiece. The hand-carved wooden leaf holds a pineapple, with artichokes, bananas, pears, grapes and crabapples grouped around it Dracaena and aralia leaves make a crescent pattern. Bamboo mat, watermelon pink napkins and wooden plates complete the luncheon table. How-to-do it drawings for making this arrangement are shown on page 118. Arranged by Anabel Combs Lasker. (Photo by Gottscho-Schleisner)*

the smooth store candle. On the warm wax, you can shape petals and flowers, ridges and valleys.

For harvesttime set a few acorns in hot wax around the base of a candle to carry a seasonal note. The same can be done with pine cones at Christmas. Gild the cones, or rub in bronzing powder with cotton wads. Sparkling ornate holiday candles, appropriate with Louis XVI and other ornate periods, can be made by pinning sequins to candles or by dripping a coat of wax on candles and adding glitter dust while the wax is still warm.

Though flower candles, especially appropriate at Easter, are expensive, they can be copied for pennies and decorated to match your best china or favorite flowered tablecloth. These candles are made with artificial flowers and thin florist's wire. Separate the flowers and leaves from their wire stems, and wire a leaf to each flower. Then chain them closely together, starting at the top and winding the stems together as you work. Melt white candles or paraffin, and dip the flowers quickly in and out of the wax for a thin even coating. While the flowers are still warm and soft, fasten them to the candle with straight pins, and cover each pinhead with a drop of wax.

BUFFET TABLES

For company and gala occasions—birthdays, weddings, holidays—the dining room or buffet serves as the focal point. Its beauty, uniqueness, and suitability will make the food seem special, the party more memorable. Special holiday settings and flowers for the rest of the house are suggested in Chapter VIII.

A floral design for a buffet table against the wall should have a wide silhouette in proportion to the space behind it. Since the buffet may be set elsewhere than in the dining room, it should reflect the spirit of the room and, in fact, can do much to carry out the decorating scheme. Determine what you want to serve, and start from there. If the pièce de résistance is served from a chafing dish, achieve balance by placing a large arrangement or serving dish at the other end of the table. The two large appointments, however, must be in scale and proportion to the table and to one another.

110.   *Even a tray meal can honor a guest. On a Chippendale table, fine Copeland china (India Tree pattern) and a Victorian Parian hand holding fragrant sweetheart roses and heather make an appealingly feminine setting. Arranged by Esther Wheeler. (Photo by Gottscho-Schleisner)*

111.   *A buffet table for a late supper features gray linen cloth, orange napkins, black pottery, and a brown casserole. The technique for making a modern long-lasting seed collage is given on page 127. Birds hung on the wall complete the circle of the design. The chafing dish on the left is balanced by the carafe on the right. Arranged by Anabel Gombs Lasker. (Photo by Gottscho-Schleisner)*

TERRACE OR PATIO TABLES AND TRAY MEALS

For a sea-food meal served on your terrace, wash and dry an empty lobster shell for a container. Place a pincup behind it, and arrange pink gladiolus and podocarpus in it. Add a few lemons or limes for accent. A repetition of the potted plant material used to border your terrace, such as an arrangement of aspidistra leaves with potted plants of aspidis-

tra, will quickly unify table and outdoor settings. Interesting wooden plates and serving dishes can be used for textural relationship.

For outdoor settings, you can use your imagination cleverly, though always keeping accessories and decorations in harmony. A busy hostess had been gardening all day to beautify her garden setting for a neighborhood gathering that evening. Her decoration was a gardening glove, the fingers stuffed with cotton and appearing to hold a dahlia,

112. *A buffet for a chicken dinner on a country terrace is decorated with twin arrangements of ivy, peppers, onions and geraniums grouped around metal roosters. One is placed on the glass top, the other on the plant stand below it. Gay ceramic plates, a wooden salad bowl, ceramic casserole and wicker ware complete the textured setting. Arranged by Anabel Combs Lasker. (Photo by Gottscho-Schleisner)*

which was in a salt shaker of water concealed behind the glove. Beside the glove was a garden trowel. Two country designs, always popular for informal decoration, are shown in Plate 112.

For a patio party, you might set four tables with different cloths, pink, yellow, pale green, and lilac. Arrange your flowers in simple designs in colors to match the cloth, deep pink and rose for the pink table, yellow daisies for the yellow table, and so on. At a large buffet, have a large floral decoration that embraces all flowers and colors.

113.   *Beauty and function go hand-in-hand in this design. A modern carafe and crystal bowl are accessories, and pink rubrum lilies arranged in a pincup are the flowers. The serving pieces can be removed when needed without disturbing the flower design. Arranged by Anabel Combs Lasker. (Photo by Gottscho-Schleisner)*

In some homes, television is a pivotal activity. Delightful plate suppers or snacks are served on coffee tables or nests of tables or trays that can be decorated with small and stable arrangements. A little pewter mug filled with garden flowers, cheerful pansies floating in an ash tray, or a bowl of fruit can highlight such a meal.

PRACTICAL POINTERS FOR PERIOD FLAVOR

The following general rules will apply to all your table settings.

1. A tablecloth should have a drop of 15 to 18 inches. Allow 26 to 30 inches for each place setting.

2. Napkins are placed left of the fork or on a service plate.

3. Your table composition should occupy less than one-third the length of the table.

The arrangement in Plate 114 is illustrated here in a possible setting. Sunlight sparkling on glass, fresh green foliage in the background, and tinkling water, would create a delighful outdoor scene. To match the color of the lilies, pink lemonade could be the beverage in the carafe.

114.   A heavy-textured jardiniere holds a long-lasting arrangement of squash, limes, green grapes and gray-green echeveria, combined with a few southern magnolia leaves in a decoration suitable for a stone column on a dining terrace. An arrangement which is not placed against a wall must be finished on all sides. Arranged by Mrs. Donald Uebelacker. (Photo by Hugelmeyer)

115. *A terrace table set in shades of brown and green includes brown wooden place mats, dull green soup bowls, and a ceramic bird in shades of green. Dried yucca, coconut sheaf, okra pods and a coconut shell contribute tan and brown. Fresh-cut succulents add interest. A pincup holds the plant material which is covered with a coconut sheaf to hide mechanics. Brown bone-handled cutlery and a tan woven rug under the table complete this exciting table. Arranged by Mrs. A. O. Samuels. (Photo by Boutrelle-Sevecke)*

4. You may place a floral or fruit and vegetable decoration in the center of your table, at the center back, or at the ends of the table, provided it is balanced with other appointments or decoration.

5. Use flowers to unify your table and dining area.

SUGGESTED TABLES FOR PERIOD FLAVOR

The following suggestions for harmonizing cloth, china, silver, glassware, and decoration should help you work out correct combinations with your own accessories. If you are planning to make new purchases, you may perhaps study these or similar combinations in fine chinaware departments of local stores.

French Elegance, Chinoiserie

Cloth: Mats of a printed chinoiserie fabric bound in gilt or silk cording, matching napkins; or lace cloth with Chinese pattern tinted to pick up one color in china, matching napkins

China: fine china in oriental pattern

Silver: Gorham Chantilly

Glass: Gold-banded goblet or clear glass stemware

Decoration: Mother-of-pearl shell, floating water lilies or peonies

116. *A hanging copper tea kettle is the container for this conversation-making table decoration. It is filled with pink geraniums and ivy. Below, bananas, grapes and kumquats add the fragrance of fruit. Arranged by Mrs. William Stickles. (Photo by Boutrelle-Sevecke)*

Provincial Manner
Cloth: Fine lawn or batiste edged with lace reflecting Le Barchichet Coif, fine linen napkins; or mats of challis wool with rosebuds printed on the wool, white linen napkins
China: Royal Doulton French Provincial, or dainty Limoges china
Silver: Towle French Provincial
Glass: Winding Wreath
Decoration: Flowering chestnut branches, tulips, roses, stock, and delphinium in fine china or bronze container

French Provincial
Cloth: Chalk-white linen cloth with rope trimming of terra cotta, wine red, or slate blue, linen napkins to match trimming; or mats of toile de Jouy print, white linen napkins
China: Pewter plates
Silver: Jensen stainless steel
Glass: Pewter goblets, crackleware, or amber glass

Decoration: Pewter or brass container with apples, wheat, herbs, and poppies

Georgian Eighteenth Century
Cloth: Green handkerchief linen, matching napkins
China: Wedgwood Charnwood
Silver: Gorham English Gadroon
Glass: Heisey or Oxford
Decoration: Roses, graded in size, with snapdragons in silver bowl

Early American—Inspired by Herb Garden
Cloth: Coarse tan linen mats with black braid or brown fringed cloth, matching napkins
China: Poppytrails, or Homestead Provincial
Silver: Reed and Barton Classic Fashion
Glass: Heisey Provincial
Decoration: Arrangement of geraniums and herbs in wicker basket

Autumn Harvest
Cloth: Yellow ocher basket-weave cloth, matching napkins; or mats of Provincial small-pattern wallpaper, Scotch-taped over cardboard, brown napkins
China: Enoch Woods Rural Scene
Silver: Reed and Barton Pointed Antique
Glass: Imperial Cape Cod
Decoration: Wheat, fruit, vegetables, and chrysanthemums in brass or copper containers

Square Dance
Cloth: Gay red and white checked cloth, white napkins
China: White Ironstone
Silver: Jensen stainless steel
Glass: Imperial Milk Glass
Decoration: Red cockscomb and apples in ironstone container

Early American Quilting Party
Cloth: Mats of printed and solid-color cotton sewed together to simulate a patchwork quilt, gay red or yellow napkins
China: California pottery Provincial
Silver: Stainless steel
Glass: Imperial Cape Cod
Decoration: Yellow and white daisies in wooden measure with liner

117. *Summer flowers arranged in a cone-shaped metal container are a delightful sur-prise to luncheon guests seated under a colorful umbrella. The container has a ring which can be hooked onto the ribs of the umbrella. Courtesy Flower Grower. (Photo by Boutrelle-Sevecke)*

Williamsburg

Cloth: Turquoise damask with matching napkins
China: Copeland India Tree
Silver: Reed and Barton Marlborough
Glass: Waterford, Alana, Lismore
Decoration: Oriental container with flowering branches and white peonies, chrysanthemums or roses according to season

American Empire

Cloth: Pale yellow damask, matching napkins
China: Rosenthal Golden Grail
Silver: Reed and Barton's Silver Wheat
Glass: Seneca Astri
Decoration: Bronze container on black marble pedestal, gilded or silvered wheat, white stock and yellow lilies, green foliage

In Victorian Mood

Cloth: Green sateen with white fringe, white napkins
China: Westmoreland Milk Glass
Silver: Gorham Buttercup or Reed and Barton Tara
Glass: Westmoreland goblets
Decoration: Yellow and white roses and carnations in a silver compote

Pacific Southwest—Inspired by Citrus Colors

Cloth: Gaily colored mats of linen, plastic, or woven materials in orange, lemon, or lime, matching napkins
China: Red Wing Tampico
Silver: Gorham Camellia
Glass: Crackleware glass in green or lime
Decoration: Wooden tray with citrus fruits, philodendron leaves, and gladiolus

Contemporary Oriental

Cloth: Grass cloth Scotch-taped to silent pad, or natural tan to pale yellow bamboo mats, yellow napkins
China: Flintridge, Marquis Coupe
Silver: Gorham Stardust or Jensen Parallel
Glass: Clear-glass footed tumbler, gray tumbler, amber crackleware
Decoration: Modern composition of black figures, cut palm leaves, and yellow chrysanthemums on black stand

Swedish

Cloth: Mats of blue, purple, and white textured weave, or gray linen cloth, with blue, purple or white napkins
China: Rostrand East Indies
Silver: Jensen Pyramid
Glass: Swedish glass
Decoration: Blue cornflowers in earthen bowl

Tropical Feeling

Cloth: Rough-woven brown straw mats or green linen cloth with brown napkins
China: Wooden plates
Silver: Towle South Wind
Glass: Crackleware
Decoration: Palm spathe containing clivia flowers with tropical foliage

The Modern Manner

Cloth: Oval mats of white plastic or black linen cloth, white napkins
China: Rosenthal Sunburst
Silver: Reed and Barton Silver Sculpture
Glass: Black, Starr & Gorham Legacy
Decoration: White or yellow calla lilies with self foliage in modern black glass container

Painter's Paradise

Cloth: Coral pink cloth or mats shaped like leaves in leafgreen linen, matching napkins
China: Hallcraft pottery in Golden Umber
Silver: Reed and Barton Pointed Antique
Glass: Crackleware
Decoration: Brown driftwood, pink torch ginger, and bananas

VIII

For holidays and other occasions

HOLIDAY DECORATIONS THAT CONFORM TO THE design requirements of your furnishings can avoid the frequently garish or banal note of an otherwise meticulously decorated room. In this chapter are suggestions for holiday arrangements that seem appropriate for various styles of homes.

NEW YEAR'S, VALENTINE'S, AND ST. PATRICK'S DAY

For a New Year's table in a countrified setting, a cock crowing ushers in the New Year. A wire frame is the base for the bird. Strips of festive paper fringed on the edges are wound around the wire and glued. A hat and beak are stapled to the bird. For a more formal setting, a collection of bells from India might be the center of interest.

Valentine's Day is an excuse for romantic and pretty parties. Lovely small bisque cupids are charming accessories for arrangements made with a few sprigs of roses and violets. The lacy quality of some replicas of Sandwich glass combined with red candlesticks and carnations make a Valentine luncheon table in the traditional manner. For dinner, try a pale pink cloth with delicate china and a dainty centerpiece of pale pink roses, a few red roses, and an accent of violets in a silver or glass container. Wire frames bent into heart shapes and wound with red or pink ribbons on opposite sides of the table can decorate a buffet.

For St. Patrick's Day, shamrock and harp motifs with early spring flowers, such as bells of Ireland, tulips, and violets, are fresh and lovely. For a humorous note in honor of the fun-loving Irish, group green leaves around a well-scrubbed potato.

EASTER—A TIME FOR FLOWERS

Lavender, green, and yellow as well as all-white reflect Easter and blend easily with most decorating schemes. Daffodils, violets, tulips, mimosa, and pussy willow are typical plant materials.

118.   *Easter is a time for flowers. A modern sculptured figurine is the central point of a formal symmetrical arrangement of calla lilies and leaves of the velvet plant. Arranged by Mrs. Godwin Stoddard. (Photo by Hugelmeyer)*

If Easter is early, steal a march on spring with forced blooms. (See Chapter V for instructions.) Apple and pear blossoms are a heavenly combination of pink and white, and azaleas give a brilliant burst of color. Andromeda japonica, an Oriental beauty, carries out modern decorating moods. Forsythia, of course, is Easter expressed in flowers and seems particularly right with Early American and Provincial fruitwoods and maple. A glass container with a generous mass of forsythia, to which a few drops of yellow food coloring have been added, is pleasing when balanced on either side with pewter candlesticks.

For the children, Easter means bunnies and eggs, and in the family room and nursery such Easter arrangements will charm the young. On a brass tray arrange a chocolate bunny, pussy willows, pink snapdragons and carnations along with eggs dyed green, pink, and brown to blend with this design. Or fill Easter baskets with flowers rather than just the straw paper and candies of tradition.

In the hall, make an arrangement that is a

119.   *Where elegance is appropriate, consider gleaming gold accents. For this Thanksgiving table, a pair of brown and gold scales below a gilded barometer on the wall hold an analogous arrangement of chrysanthemums from bronzy gold to deep orange. Gold pheasants as accessories repeat the design in the white and beige plates. The beige cloth harmonizes with the band on the plates. Arranged by Anabel Combs Lasker. (Photo by Gottscho-Schleisner)*

celebration of returning spring, with the re-creation of a bit of woodland, daffodils and pussy willows in driftwood, or tulips, snap-dragons, and pussy willow.

In a Federal or Directoire room, a white alabaster urn holding lilies and funkia foliage has ancient symbolism, since the lily was a flower of Grecian mythology.

For Easter tables, make cloths of felt, or-gandy, fiberglas, or linen. Painted wire bas-kets filled with decorated Easter eggs placed on either side of an arrangement of spring flowers are lovely. Another Easter table has a mauve cloth of felt or silk fiber to set the holiday pace. White clear crystal and lettuce green, pink, or yellow pottery plates carry out the Easter note. A centerpiece of pussy willow, daffodils, tulips, or hyacinths in colors of pink, yellow, or lavender are arranged in a massed effect in a gilded basket. Ceramic bunnies used as accessories complete this table.

MAY HOLIDAYS AND INDEPENDENCE DAY

Mother's Day, Father's Day, June brides and graduations are all occasions for celebration. Table and other decorations may take their cue from the personality of the person hon-ored. While traditional carnations or roses in crystal may express sweet and treasured memories of Mother's Day, the personalities of contemporary parents may be developed thematically through the use of more modern arrangements. Father's Day, for example, may be celebrated with an arrangement of porcelain ducks placed against a background of unpretentious field grasses and daisies in a bamboo container. Or a table for Father's Day can use the colors of leaf green, brown, gray, or blue. Try making table mats of syn-

120. *A doorway is decorated with a cone basket containing fresh-cut carnations with heather for luck! Instructions on page 174. Arranged by Esther Wheeler. (Photo by Gottscho-Schleisner)*

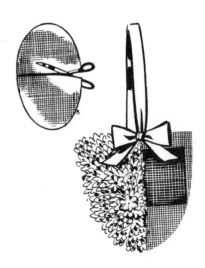

thetic leather, bamboo, or tweedy textured wall coverings and have harmonizing pottery, pewter, or wooden plates. A centerpiece might feature a figurine typical of Dad's favorite hobby with seasonal flowers, such as daisies, cornflowers, delphiniums, and evergreens.

A beautiful Mother's Day table covering can be made of wallpaper Scotch-taped over your silent pad or in mat form. This opens a wide field to choose from. If Mother is sophisticated and modern, use marbleized wallpaper. (Matching plates in marbleized finish are available.) Use clear crystal and a centerpiece built around a figurine of classic beauty using ti leaves with white gladiolus or calla lilies with self foliage. If Mother prefers homespun textures, cover the table pad with Provincial printed paper in small pattern. Use dull slate blue, gray, or tan linen napkins and harmonizing pottery plates, and as container, a homemaker's implement, a rolling pin, sewing basket, bean pot, casserole, or trivet. A pincup can hold the water. Flowers such as sweet-scented geraniums, daisies, or mixed garden flowers, or a vegetable arrangement make a quaint table decoration.

Fourth of July celebrations are often held outdoors. Picnic tables as well as indoor dining-room tables can feature patriotic settings combining vivid red cloths, white china, and blue napkins with an arrangement of white and red carnations and purple-blue iris.

THANKSGIVING DECORATIONS

Thanksgiving, the family feast day, lends itself to arrangements of fruits and vegetables. Where pine and maple predominate, rough-textured and uneven forms have a homespun quality. Try squash, zucchini, Indian corn, peppers, and garden chrysanthemums in a wooden salt box, copper pitcher, or breadbasket. Such an arrangement should last for weeks.

A seasonal decoration of dried materials in gold, brown, yellow, green, orange, or purple might be arranged in an old wooden butter bowl to pick up the colors in a French Provincial or Early American room.

For a small room in the Empire tradition, in which elegance is the prevailing mood, combine grapes in hues that range from green to russet violet, placed in black marble urns, the pair of urns on pedestals of different heights, so that the grapes in the upper urn seem to cascade to the lower one.

121. *Inside the door, a gay felt Christmas tree hangs. Instructions on page 178. Arranged by Mrs. John G. McReynolds. (Photo by Gottscho-Schleisner)*

122. *(Left)* *For an Early American den, the Christmas decoration is an arrangement of pine and red carnations in an antique bedwarmer. Arranged by Esther Wheeler. (Photo by Gottscho-Schleisner)*

123. *A French Provincial mantel with Provence figurines and candlesticks, holds twin floral arrangements in pincups placed behind angels. Chrysanthemums and leucothoë, in tints and tones of red to red-orange, are a change from Christmas red and green. Arranged by Anabel Combs Lasker. (Photo by Gottscho-Schleisner)*

From a color point of view, Thanksgiving decorations are ideally suited to many modern homes. Dried materials, such as cattails and dock, milkweed pods and mullein, offer varieties of textural contrast along with autumn leaves and chrysanthemums and asters. Also, harvest arrangements afford an excellent opportunity for analogous color schemes and are suitable for contemporary rooms where the stress is on wood and nubby materials.

Indian corn wired together with a few autumn leaves makes a pleasing wall decoration in the right surroundings, as in a pine-paneled study or on a fireplace wall.

For young children, the whole drama of the first Thanksgiving can be re-enacted through flower arrangements. Around a small stone symbolizing Plymouth Rock, group other symbols of the first harvest—Indian corn, pumpkins, barley, and bayberry foliage. Use candy figurines as Pilgrim accessories.

For the playroom, sun porch, or other informal area, you might make an arrangement in a hollowed pumpkin shell. A bowl of water inserted in the shell keeps the plant material fresh. Combine such materials as dried corn tassels and leaves, red sumac seed cones, canna foliage, and rust chrysanthemums.

THANKSGIVING TABLE SETTINGS

These suggested Thanksgiving table settings will help you to visualize the required harmony between accessories and decoration.

Cloth: Tangerine broadcloth, chartreuse napkins
China: Stangl Fruit Ring
Silver: Gorham Nocturne
Glass: Heavy modern crystal
Decoration: Two bamboo stands (the smaller one placed on top of the other) on which, piled high, are black and green grapes, orange persimmons, russet pears, green avocados, and orange kumquats with their own foliage

Cloth: Gray metallic fabric, matching napkins
China: Special turkey plates
Silver: Gorham Lyric
Glass: Smoked gray goblets with gold rims
Decoration: Horn of plenty surrounded by fruits

Cloth: Brown linen, matching napkins
China: Red Wing Capistrano
Silver: Gorham Old French
Decoration: Grouping of black grapes, green artichokes, green peppers, and purple plums on unstained board of pecky cypress

EXTERIOR CHRISTMAS DECORATIONS

Christmas decorations are a potpourri of customs from many lands, easily adapted to today's living. While many of us like to follow traditional decorations and a color scheme of bright red and green, you may find that decorations that harmonize with your home décor in color and design are especially pleasing. Therefore you can make "Something a little different" a holiday rule for your next Christmas.

Outdoor decorations can suit the architecture and colors of your house as do your indoor decorations. Use your knowledge and understanding of decorating periods in your exterior decorations. For a ranch house done in the modern manner, make a swag of several large pieces of evergreen to which can be attached one large brown cone. In the center of the swag, attach a bow of fresh aspidistra leaves that have been sprayed lightly with gold.

For a traditional house, hang a cone basket outside filled with fresh flowers and evergreens. To make a cone basket, cut an oval of hardware cloth 24 inches long and 16 inches wide. Then cut the oval into two pieces so that each piece measures 12 inches high and 16 inches wide. Completely cover one piece with white pine cones, attaching them with

124. *(Right)   Make a special tree for your little girl or hers! This one, of green Punchinello ribbon (see instructions for making it on this page) holds tiny toys. Arranged by Esther Wheeler. (Photo by Gottscho-Schleisner)*

125. *(Center)   "Merry Christmas to all . . ." A Christmas punch table uses a red circular cloth with heavy fringe and napkins to match. The appointments are a large glass punch bowl and goblets. Holly and white carnations nestle in a white wire candelabra and the punch bowl is encircled in holly. Arranged by Mrs. James L. Finch. (Photo by Boutrelle-Sevecke)*

126. *(Bottom)   "Bearing gifts we traverse afar." Camels tell the Christmas story. Instructions for making the chinaberry wreath on page 178. Topiary roosters courtesy of W. & J. Sloane. Wreath arranged by Esther Wheeler. (Photo by Gottscho-Schleisner)*

wire to the small openings in the hardware cloth and tying the wires in the back. Spray the cones with copper or gold bronzing liquid, and sprinkle them with glitter while wet. Fasten this piece to the undecorated piece so that the decoration is the shape of half an oval, leaving an opening at the straight top for a liner to hold flowers. The handle can be made of copper or green ribbon. Add water to the liner, and fill with fresh flowers and evergreens. (See Plate 120.)

EXTERIOR CHRISTMAS WREATHS

Traditional houses and Christmas wreaths are a natural combination, and the wreath can fit the architecture of the house.

To make a wreath, you will require a stout pair of pruning shears and a wire cutter. Bend two coat hangers into a circle, or twist the branches from a willow tree or forsythia bush into a circle if you want a larger wreath. Clip the evergreens you have gathered into short even lengths, about 6 inches. Start at the top of the frame, and work down on the left side, binding the material to the frame with green wire about 20-gage. Take several pieces of evergreen in your left hand, and bind them tightly to the frame with the stems at the center and the tips at the outside. Continue this, alternating with the twig tips toward the inside. Overlap the material closely, and when you have reached the center bottom, hang the wreath on a nail, and step back to see if you have worked evenly. Continue on the right side of the wreath until the evergreens meet and overlap.

A Georgian house forms a good backdrop for a della Robbia wreath made of fruit shellacked to vivid brightness and wired, each piece separately, to the wreath. Small fruits,

such as kumquats, lemons, limes, and lady apples, and pears, are wired individually, and bright red cranberries are wired in small bunches stuck on toothpicks. Pine cones are also wired into this wreath arrangement, with the different colors framed against a background of green.

INDOOR WREATHS FOR CHRISTMAS

Indoor wreaths are very decorative. In a formal living room with paneled walls, such as Empire or Federal, wreaths constructed of shellacked or silvered ivy leaves wired onto 8-inch circles are handsome, especially when used in sets of three or more.

A friendship wreath makes an interesting centerpiece for a large coffee table or a modern buffet in pickled pine. Cut an octagonal form out of cardboard, 14 inches in diameter. Inside of this, cut an 8-inch circle. Cover with lightweight burlap that has been sprayed with gold. Buy a 10-inch sphagnum wreath from your florist. Place on the wreath with wire picks pieces of dried material such as seed pods and cones. Attach the wreath to the burlap foundation. You may have collected the seed pods on vacation trips or received them from friends near and far throughout the years; for example, Eucalyptus pods and pepper berries from California, piñon cones from the Northwest, cotton blossoms and peanuts from the South, sweet-gum balls from the Midwest, pine cones from Maine, and the largest acorns imaginable from Texas. In the center of this wreath, place a modern carved wooden Madonna.

A boxwood wreath, especially appropriate for a room in French décor, may be made by wiring boxwood onto a frame of three sturdy sticks. The inside of the frame should be

127.   In this French Provincial dining room a fruitwood table is set with ivory linen place mats and matching napkins, embroidered in gold thread. The centerpiece is nostalgic of a Christmas in France: a piece of bark holding fruits and pine cones, and a pot of pink cyclamen. Arranged by Esther Wheeler, in the home of Rosanna Wheeler.(Photo by Gottscho-Schleisner)

circular and the outside triangular. It may be decorated with shellacked kumquats, small lady apples, and pine cones. It should not measure more than 9 inches around.

An upright wreath of chinaberries, as in Plate 126, may be placed in a window, flanked by carved wooden camels. To make a chinaberry wreath, cover an 18-inch ring by winding it first with cotton and then with gold ribbon. Wind the stems of the berries around this covered ring. Substitutes for chinaberries can be whitened hemlock cones, cotton blossoms, or similar material. Make the wreath stand upright by nailing the bottom part to a heavy block. Let the three camels relate the decoration to the Christmas season.

MANTEL DECORATIONS

Mantels are the natural focus for Christmas decorations, and there are many lovely ideas to try in keeping with your décor. A French Provincial room, as in Plate 123, might have Provence figurines and candlesticks with twin floral arrangements of chrysanthemums and leucothoë ranging in tints and tones from red to red-orange.

For a modern home that has a mantel with a large mirror, make this wreath. Cut 4-inch pieces of silver Punchinello ribbon. Wire them onto a 12-inch ring by attaching the middle of each 4-inch piece of ribbon to the ring with wire until the ring is completely covered and very full. Flank the wreath with crystal candlesticks.

For a classic mantel, an Adam or a Georgian, a lady-apple swag is beautiful. Make a simple wooden frame shaped like a broad H, and tack wire mesh over it for attaching a background of cedar, yew, or balsam. With the background complete, insert clumps of juniper and coned spruce sprays, and add lacquered lady apples, crab apples, cones, and even clumps of gilded peanuts. Decorate it with bows. If your room has gold accents, spray the swag lightly with gold.

For decorating an Early American or colonial fireplace with a natural finish wood mantel, place a pewter bowl filled with holly and evergreen far to one side. As an accessory use a Madonna against a pewter plate.

NOVEL CHRISTMAS TREES

You can make interesting table trees that will carry out your room décor. In a small elegant room, for example, a table tree of succulents and red berries wired onto a mesh cone has a soft velvety look, with red berries impaled on toothpicks for accent. The succulents can be planted when holidays are over.

Table trees may also be made in the same way as the succulent tree, with the cone of wire supported by a dowel "planted" in a flowerpot.

For your kitchen, spray a small tree with red paint, and hang kitchen utensils on it for decoration.

For inside a door or outside a closet door, make a green felt Christmas tree, 36 inches high and 24 inches at the base, pinking the edges, and trimming the tree with sequins and beads. Add carved wooden Italian angels for distinction. Drape the tree with gold trimming and sequins. Sew a felt pot onto the tree at the bottom. The tree can also be trimmed by sewing on it buttons and jewelry from your trinket box.

For a child's room, make a little tree of Punchinello ribbon. For an 18-inch tree, cut a circle measuring 36 inches in diameter out

128. *"Dreaming of a White Christmas!" A white pine wreath hangs at the window of this typical Early American kitchen. Driftwood, painted white and dusted with iridescent sequins while still wet, holds a Santa made of a styrofoam ball impaled on a red funnel. Sequins make the eyes, ears and nose. White styrofoam balls rest on a few branches of pine which relate the table composition to the wreath. Arranged by Esther Wheeler, in the home of Rosanna Wheeler. (Photo by Gottscho-Schleisner)*

of hardware cloth. Divide it into quarters, and use a quarter of this circle for the cone shape of the tree. On a spool of wire, ruffle about 10 yards of Punchinello ribbon, threading the wire through the center of the ribbon. The fuller the ruffle, the better-looking the tree will be. Spiral the ruffle around the cone tree until it is completely covered, then fasten it. Trim the tree with miniature toys,

and place it on a small table covered with a trimmed circular corduroy mat. (See Plate 125.)

OTHER CHRISTMAS IDEAS

For a room in the classic tradition, use an urn arrangement of greens and cones that are

129. *"Home for Christmas." A gay decoration of potted Christmas gift plants, white poinsettias, peperomia obtusifolia variegata, dieffenbachia, and watermelon pink cyclamen. Sponge rubber coasters are placed under pots. In the home of Rosanna Wheeler. (Photo by Gottscho-Schleisner)*

supported in crumpled wire. Fleck them with glitter.

For a modern room, use whitewashed broom or branches of magnolia grandiflora. Place them in a black narrow-necked vase, and trim them with colored Christmas balls. Whitewashed rhododendron leaves may be substituted.

For a coffee table in a formal living room, make a large "poinsettia" by painting magnolia grandiflora (or any large flat leaf), and spray with canned snow while the paint is wet. When dry, thread the leaves at the base with fine wire, and coil around a piñon cone. Touch up the cone with glue and glitter, and place the flower on a slab of wood.

ANNIVERSARIES MARKED WITH FLOWERS

Anniversaries offer an opportunity to let the imagination run riot with clever motifs of wood, glass, silver, and gold. For an amusing paper anniversary table design, make table mats of cardboard with mementos of the wedding. Fit into a pattern on each cardboard such items as thank-you letters, match covers, napkins, announcements, bits of decoration from parties celebrating the wedding, or travel brochures from the honeymoon. After gluing these mementos on the mats, cover them with lacquer.

For an anniversary table for Mother and Dad, feature one of the colorful glasswares from Mother's collection—cranberry, Tiffany, pressed glass, vaseline or Sandwich. Let the glass itself suggest your color range. Tiffany glass, for example, is popular again and is just as striking in a modern room as in a period one. Combine it with modern textured table covering, or perhaps light brown, gold, or blue mats or cloth. Select brown lusterware plates and flecked gold modern ware to flatter a centerpiece of fine flowers in a Tiffany or bronze container. Roses are especially beautiful in Tiffany glass, as are peonies, snapdragons, or chrysanthemums. Each would be appropriate according to season.

A Victorian room might have a table set as in Plate 130 for a golden wedding. The gray rayon cloth reproduces an old one, and the reproduction ironstone china is Franklin with diamond-patterned goblets. An old alabaster urn holds marigolds, roses, ferns, and grapes.

FLOWER DECORATIONS FOR WEDDINGS

Home wedding parties can be made especially significant with decorations to honor the occasion. A party for the bride can be worked out in feminine pink, icy blue, and snowy white. If the occasion is a shower, the decorations can be placed in containers that are also gifts, the centerpiece a gift casserole filled with roses or a frying pan filled with bronzy chrysanthemums.

For the wedding itself, obtain a roping of smilax from your florist for draping mantels and stairways. If it is a spring wedding, bank the fireplace and each side of the mantel with branches of spring blossoms, such as apple and crab apple. Decorate the mantel with a large arrangement of white flowers. Arrange miniature roses, Pour Toi, in small glass china shoes for the guest tables, which can be covered with pastel cloths to carry out your color scheme.

Flower arrangements can be made the day before the wedding and kept in a cool place.

130.   *Polish up the silver for a 25th Anniversary party! The table is set with exquisite lace mats and runners, and fine Minton china. Etched Bristol candlesticks with silver decoration repeat the silver of china and goblets. Roses, snapdragons and chrysanthemums are arranged in a crescent design. Arranged by Anabel Combs Lasker, in the home of Mrs. Harry Fine. (Photo by Gottscho-Schleisner)*

131. A dinner table set for a Golden Wedding uses reproductions of Victorian appointments: a gray nylon tablecloth simulating the fine linen damask cloths of earlier days; Franklin china; a copy of old ironstone with a Chinese pattern; and goblets which are replicas of a Sandwich glass in a diamond pattern. To complete this "remembrance of things past" an antique alabaster urn holds an arrangement of red-orange marigolds, yellow roses, sprengeri fern and grapes. Arranged by Esther Wheeler. (Photo by Richard Averill Smith)

When they are finally placed, all that is needed is a little touch-up, such as an extra flower or leaf. Through the use of correct containers and the choice of design and color, wedding decorations will fit into your home decorating style. Thus for a wedding in a modern house, heavy-cut crystal of contemporary design should be used with roses, tulips, and gladiolus.

A suggestion about wedding flowers. Stiffness through the use of too many spiked forms, such as gladiolus or huckleberry foliage, detracts from the effect. Cut the spikes in different lengths.

The wedding table can be as simple or spectacular as the family wishes. One trend is away from all white toward accents of pale yellow, pink, or blue. Study your foliage. You can obtain beautiful effects with white flowers and gray foliage. Usually the wedding cake dominates the table, and if so, it can be surrounded by a wreath of gardenias. An elegant and timesaving wreath can be made ahead of time by silvering dried magnolia grandiflora leaves, or ivy. However, if space allows, have the wedding cake by itself on a small round table covered with net with a liner of satin. Loop ropings of smilax to the edge of the table. Around the edge fasten corsages of white carnations to form a carnation circle, placing the decorated cake in the center.

For a contemporary home, an elegant centerpiece for a bridesmaid's table uses a French

132.   *A bridesmaids' table uses a chartreuse cloth and napkins and pressed-glass plates and goblets as a foil for the rich reds and blues in the Royal Doulton and Whieldon figurines. The centerpiece unifies the setting with dark red snapdragons, red carnations and pale pink roses with chartreuse viburnum foliage. Arranged by Esther Wheeler. (Photo by Boutrelle-Sevecke)*

compote, filled with snapdragons, lilacs, and peonies, as shown in Plate 131. Another contemporary decoration with flowers is a hanging wall arrangement to complement a bride's table, as shown in Plate 133. The table centerpiece combines lily of the valley with Fugi chrysanthemums.

A wedding table for an informal room may have dotted Swiss or embroidered organdy for a table covering, milk glass plates and goblets, and white geraniums for decoration. A charming Victorian table may be set with an old lace cloth and an arrangement of white roses, bouvardia, and maidenhair fern. In a modern room, the feeling of décor can be captured with calla lilies, gardenias, or white anthurium smartly arranged in clear crystal containers and used with textured white and silver cloths.

134. *Whatever the holiday or party occasion, you can create an ambiance with just a few flowers and interesting accessories. Here several anemones and carnations in low bowls set the stage for lovely porcelain figures. Notwithstanding the simplicity of the arrangement, it has elegance and style. Designed by and in the home of Mrs. Albert D. Lasker.*

IX

The garden room

IN THE TWELVE YEARS SINCE THIS BOOK WAS first published, there have been many changes in general attitudes towards plants. Interest in rule-bound flower arrangement has declined but, on the other hand, almost everyone wants to grow *something*. A garden has always been a symbol of the good life. Today it—and its counterpart, the garden room—is also an escape valve that eases some of the pressures of mechanized living.

The farmlands of yesterday are the Levittowns of today, apartment houses tower in the suburban scene; in the city, those grace notes that we called foyers and entrance halls and dressing rooms are now rented as half-rooms. Naturally, then, every inch of space must count. Dual-purpose rooms are the trend, and we convert sun porches and basements to garden living rooms; we convert unused back-

yards by adding greenhouses, lanais, and atriums; in the city, we create tiny gardens in window sills or bookcases, as antidotes to the aridity of concrete-steeel-glass life.

In the photos which follow we try to show you some of the newest trends in creating better living space. Note the stress on architectural features such as pilasters, beams, columns, on multi-level floors which divide living areas and bring spacious movement and excitement to the simple rectangle that was the room of the past. And note, by all means, that everywhere in these rooms of the present and the future, plants abound!

Plates 135 through 140 demonstrate our statement that a basement can be just a hole in the ground—or a marvelous place for family gatherings.

135. (Left) This basement is worth dropping by for! It was enlivened with pebbles embedded in concrete, and built-in planters that make foliages seem to spring directly from the floor. A skylight four stories up supplies needed light. In the open central staircase, the garden can be seen from all upper levels. Designed by architect Carl Strauss.

136. (Below) Molded concrete blocks which edge the planting, masonry walls, heavily-carved wood and strongly-textured foliage all have a design affinity that engages and pleases the eye. The artificial lights built into the basement window supply a necessity for plant growth. (Courtesy Rees and Orr Inc.)

137. (Left) The support column in the basement was covered with mosaic tiles and used as a focus for a circular planter at its base. Garden furniture brings the look of outdoors to a one-time cellar. (Courtesy Scroll Aluminum)

138. *(Left)* *Groupings of plants soften the abrupt change in levels in a split-level house. Designed by Lord & Taylor. (Courtesy Amtico)*

139. *(Right)* *A windowless family room acquires a light and airy feeling thanks to a trellis made of lath strips. The fabric canopy draped on rods conceals the overhead pipes and is repeated in the upholstering. The ferns in pots pick up the fabric motif; ray forms in the painting are repeated in the fresh daisy petals. Designed by Ellen L. McCluskey, F.A.I.D. (Courtesy Amtico)*

140. (Above)   The potato cellar in a barn has been converted into a child's summer bedroom. Vines trail from the tile-covered wall and spill out from a horse trough. The spiral staircase wends down from the first floor. Designed by Gina Beadle.

141 (Left)   Plants of unusual shape that seem to crawl, creep, twine and invade space in striking three-dimensional ways were chosen as foils for the static flatness of the glass expanse. The effect is arresting and dramatic.

142. *(Right) Floral colors can be both asset and seasonal indicator: potted tulips and azaleas make a pleasant springtime doorway decoration just outside a home office; in the summer petunias and geraniums signal the change in season. The concrete block planter is decorative and, as it retains moisture, practical as well.*

143. *(Below) To hang something above eye level is to give it immediate importance. In this garden room created by enclosing a breezeway, choice begonias are grown in suspended planters and in containers set into the border. Designed by architect Fred Langhorst. (Courtesy California Redwood Association)*

144. *(Right) Repetition as an art principle is discussed in Chapter IV, but noteworthy here is the large scale of the dracaena, whose leaves repeat the art nouveau design in the armoire. This exaggeration of scale is a current trend. (Courtesy Directional)*

There's less space around these days, so every foot of it must count. The half-garden rooms shown in plate numbers 145 through 147 are functional, but they are pretty as well, for in each of them a corner or a wall has been given over to plants.

145. (Above) A built-in cabinet under the pitched window of a cool green-and-white study has space for storage below, and a recessed counter for potted plants on top. Designed by Tom Woods, A.I.D. (Courtesy Bigelow-Sanford, Inc.)

146. In this home office, cacti and succulents (in clay pots which are both decorative and functional) create balance for the shelf wall, and require little care. Designed by Rhoda Bright, N.S.I.D. (Courtesy Amtico)

147. (Right) Palms, ferns, podocarpus and chrysanthemums fill the corner void in a recreation room. The vinyl flooring is practical and makes a transitional corridor to the adjacent terrace. Designed by David Barrett, A.I.D. (Courtesy Amtico)

Ingenious planting solutions to some common architectural problems are shown in plates 148 to 154.

148. *(Left) A connecting corridor to a breezeway becomes a garden room. Plants are contained in boxes which double as low walls. Sculptured forms of driftwood are silhouetted against the gray background of the wooden breezeway. Designed by David Rhame. (Courtesy California Redwood Association)*

149. *(Below)   Service areas (this one is the garbage depot) can be screened with ornamental wood panels and plantings. (Courtesy Custom Wood Manufacturing Company)*

150. (Above) How to create a garden room out of thin air. Architect Robert Hayes built this shelter for his own home, situated on an almost vertical lot. Redwood superstructure and balustrade provide a feeling of security, harmonize with natural surroundings. The light weight of redwood makes such second-floor gardens possible. Bonsai trees, echeveria, sedum and succulents are the potted plants. (Photo by Karl Riek)

151. (Above) It could have been an awkward situation, but continuation of border plantings (and flooring) in an indoor-outdoor bed creates unity for garden room and an adjoining terrace. (Courtesy Rolscreen Company)

152. (Right) A sloping facade provides practical hinged housing for garden tools and hose, and frames the garden room as well. Designed by Tom Woods, A.I.D. (Courtesy U. S. Plywood)

153. *(Right)   Why not convert that back entrance into an atrium? If the area is enclosed (but not over-heated) it may offer ideal houseplant nursery conditions. Accessory lights and heaters on timers can make it a year-round growing area. (Courtesy Hotpoint)*

154. *(Above)   An inexpensive modernizing project for an old house uses terrace doors of sculptured wood leading to a garden room where house plants thrive in antique containers. (Courtesy Custom Wood Manufacturing Company)*

155. *(Right)   Plants and water are natural companions. In the corners of a garden room, a fountain sculpted in the shape of plants offers pleasure to eye and ear. Bubbling water is circulated by a small pump concealed in the base. The water, forced up through the stems, cascades down to the area below, then begins the cycle once again. (Courtesy Silas Seandel Studio)*

156. *(Right) Sculptures with free-form motifs from nature are superb accessories for plant rooms. (Courtesy Dr. Kaare K. Nygaard)*

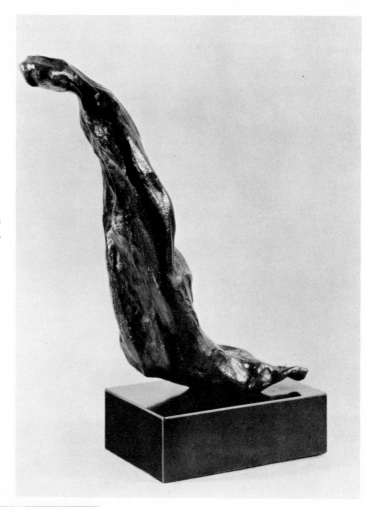

157.   *Modern-bowl, pump-equipped fountains reflect the fascination of hanging plants that frame and give depth to a small garden. The pebbles covering the ground reduce maintenance, and add to the Oriental quality of the area. (Courtesy Reasoner's Tropical Nurseries)*

158. *(Left) Plants and water again. In a well-planned enclosure for a pool, exotic plant materials are grown as decoration. The small flower bed provides a succession of blooms with fall chrysanthemums, spring bulbs, and summer annuals, in season. (Courtesy Charles R. Wedding Nurseries)*

159. *In this garden room cum sun bath, kiln-dried resawn redwood treated with a protective finish panels the bath and goes on to fence a very private garden enclosure with delicate ferns and flowers, classical statuary and liberal sunlight. Designed by architects Killingsworth and Brady.*

Rooms need boundaries,. especially outdoors. Not only to mark space but to make us feel secure, snug and secluded. Some boundaries are clear and well-defined; others are merely suggested.

160. *(Left)   Here the openwork roof is light and airy, full of shadow play and changing texture. The trellis protects the large glass windows from sun glare, ties the house to the landscaping, and still admits light and warmth in winter. Designed by architect David Leaf. (Photo by Morley Baer)*

161. *(Above)   Modules of a cluster house are connected by a deck to make a sun-filled secluded atrium, with Japanese maple and bamboo, green against the rich redwood, providing overhead screening and marking a boundary.*

162.   *The ceiling here is a picturesque welled-in tree, a natural umbrella on a patio. It shades a dining area and splash pool.*

Even where daylight is lacking you can grow an indoor gardenful of plants if you use high-intensity fluorescent lamps for 12 to 16 hours daily. You can grow poinsettias at Christmas, tulips for Valentine's Day, lilies at Easter and potted annuals all through the summer. Select plants from the following lists according to the amount of light available. (You can measure foot-candles with a photographer's light meter.)

Plants that require low light:

Minimum: 50 foot-candles
Preferred: 100 to 500 foot-candles
Aglaonema (Chinese evergreen)
Aspidistra (Iron plant)
Dieffenbachia (Dumb cane)
Dracaena
Nephthytis (Syngonium)
Pandanus vietchi (Screwpine)
Philodendron oxycardium
Philodendron pertusum (Monstera)
Sansevieria (Snakeplant)

Plants that require medium light:

Minimum: 500 foot-candles
Preferred: 1,000 foot candles
Aglaonema roebelini (Chinese evergreen)
Anthurium hybrids
Begonia metallica
Begonia rex
Bromeliads
Cissus (Grape ivy)
Ficus (Rubber plant)
Kentia Fosteriana (Kentia palm)
Peperomia
Philodendrons, other than *oxycardium*
Pilea cadieri (Aluminum plant)
Schefflera
Scindapsus Aureus

Plants that require high light:

Minimum: 1,000 foot-candles
Preferred: Above 1,000 foot-candles
Aloe variegata
Begonias, other than metallica and rex
Codiaeum
Coleus
Crassula

Episcia
Fatshedera lizei
Hedera (Ivy)
Hoya carnosa
Impatiens
Kalanchoe tomentosa
Pelargonium species (Geranium)
Petunia hybrida (Cascade type)
Saintpaulia species (African violets)
Salvia splendens (Scarlet sage)
Sinningia species (Gloxinia)
Tagetes species (Marigold)

It's best to set the plants into clay pots before you put them into your planter as you can move the pots in and out as needed to keep the garden well-groomed and attractive. Use upended clay pots as bases to raise plants so that all are at a uniform level. Fill spaces between pots with coarse gravel up to a depth of 3 or 4 inches. Then fill the rest of the box around the pots with unmilled sphagnum moss, pea-sized gravel or mable chips. Directions for care of the plants are given on page 152.

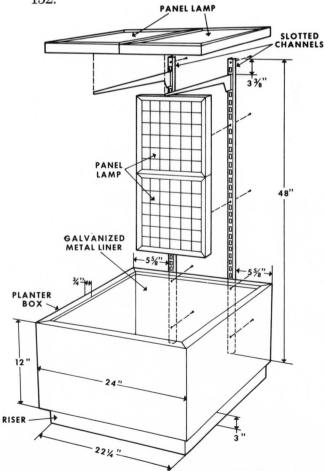

NOTE: You can judge foot candles as follows. Two forty-watt cool white fluorescents 6″ from the top of the plant will produce about 860 foot candles; 12″ from the top of the plant, 500 foot candles; 18″ from plant, 380 foot candles.

163.   *Any handyman can make this planter box following plan A (see preceding page), but be sure that a licensed electrician installs the light.*

164.   *This divided indoor gardens meets the needs of plants with differing cultural requirements. Foliage plants growing a distance from the light source need low light intensity; below the cabinet African violets, close to the fluorescent bulbs, get greater intensity.*

165. *In an area remote from windows, a pebble-lined planter in the floor holds a variety of plants, including a terrarium. Artificial light (normally blue-purple but modified here to include deluxe warm white lamps) has been built into a soffit to provide for plants' cultural needs.*

166. *An old-fashioned collection of plants in a sunny window has universal appeal, but what does one do if the window is sunless? Swivel lights, focused on the plants for at least 12 hours daily, provide an answer.*

Scan the ads in flower magazines or visit a flower show; you'll be convinced that almost everyone yearns for a greenhouse. And why not, since you can grow all kinds of plant rarities under glass. If possible, build an attached greenhouse so you won't need to brave the winter cold to get to it. Second piece of advice: Make the greenhouse twice as large as you think you need and use it as living space too.

168. *Not all greenhouses blend as happily with the existing structure as this one. Most manufacturers will help you choose materials suited to the design and construction of your house.*

167. *(Below) This greenhouse-that-was-once-a-sun-porch has plenty of space for family living. Plants take up only one wall.*

(Courtesy Lord & Burnham)

X

The placement show

MORE AND MORE GARDEN CLUBS NOW OFFER shows featuring arrangements planned for home settings. Mrs. W. H. Barton offers these suggestions for flower-show exhibits: "The thousands of people who each year throng to large and small floral exhibitions give testimony to the universal appeal of flowers, both as specimens and in arrangements.

"These shows are artistically produced and have an immense educational value. However, when staged in a residence, where actual problems of space and color must be solved, practicality is added to education and enjoyment. Because the arrangement should be correct in mood, period, size and color for its place in a room, this type of show is aptly called 'The Placement Show.' If the show is to be eligible for credit by the National Council of State Garden clubs, requirements for a Standard Show must be observed.

"One or more homes may be used and fresh cut plant material should provide the dominant design interest in the scheduled classes.

"Since the Schedule Committee is of prime importance it should be appointed with care. Each residence selected should be surveyed. The number of exhibits and their locations will be determined by the size and type of home. This Committee should know the seasonal flowers, ability of the members and by all means have vision and imagination. The vision of the Schedule Committee and the ability of the exhibitor must combine to produce an arrangement or composition which will enhance and complement its surroundings.

"Each room will be considered as a class, with at least four exhibits, the only exception to this being halls, powder rooms, etc. where one arrangement will be acceptable. Too many exhibits in any room produce a cluttered effect.

"The usual home will have at least five rooms suitable for exhibits, thus complying with Standard Show requirements. If two or more homes are used, the show will be above average quality.

"Each exhibit in the room must be point

scored with 'Suitability to Placement' receiving at least twenty-five points on the scale for judging.

"This type of show opens many homes not otherwise viewed by the public and is sometimes used as a successful fund raising project. Clubs with large membership, staging such a show, whether for profit or other objectives, prefer to exhibit a larger number of arrangements. They should require three entries for each location in the home. These exhibits should be prejudged and only the highest scoring entry shown in the place for which it was designed. The remainder may be shown elsewhere in the home on tables scheduled for exhibits failing to receive first awards.

"The Horticulture Sections may be staged in one home if enough space is available. A garage, patio, den or other suitable locations may be used. These classes should equal in number the classes in the Artistic Section.

"If more than one home is used there may be a Tricolor award offered for each home provided the entry scores over ninety-five points. Also an award of merit could be offered in the Horticulture Section to an outstanding or distinctive entry.

"Since the placement show requires cooperation in many areas of endeavor (hostesses, publicity, and such), it may utilize every member in a single club project. It demonstrates effectively the training received in a Flower Show School or may be the means of interesting prospective members in club activities."

Index